Remember This?

People, Things and Events
FROM **1956** TO THE **PRESENT DAY**

US EDITION

Rewind, Replay, Remember

What can you remember before you turned six? If you're like most of us, not much: the comforting smell of a blanket or the rough texture of a sweater, perhaps. A mental snapshot of a parent arriving home late at night. A tingle of delight or the shadow of sorrow.

But as we grow out of childhood, our autobiographical and episodic memories—they're the ones hitched to significant events such as birthdays or leaving school—are created and filed more effectively, enabling us to piece them together at a later date. And the more we revisit those memories, the less likely we are to lose the key that unlocks them.

We assemble these fragments into a more-or-less coherent account of our lives—the one we tell to ourselves, our friends, our relatives. And while this one-of-a-kind biopic loses a little definition over the years, some episodes remain in glorious technicolor—although it's usually the most embarrassing incidents!

But this is one movie that's never quite complete. Have you ever had a memory spring back unbidden, triggered by something seemingly unrelated? This book is an attempt to discover those forgotten scenes using the events, sounds, and faces linked to the milestones in your life.

It's time to blow off the cobwebs and see how much you can remember!

It Happened in 1956

The biggest event in the year is one that didn't make the front pages: you were born! Here are some of the national stories that people were talking about.

- Eisenhower and Nixon elected to 2nd term
- "Million Dollar Quartet" meet for a recording session (Elvis, Jerry Lee Lewis, Carl Perkins, and Johnny Cash)
- Boxer Rocky Marciano retires undefeated
- IBM invents first computer hard drive
- Supreme Court declares segregated busing illegal
- Actress Grace Kelly marries royalty (right)
- Teflon pans invented
- Video recorder (and video tape) developed
- Five missionaries killed in Ecuador
- United Methodist Church allows women to become clergy
- Two planes collide over Grand Canyon
- Dean Martin & Jerry Lewis end their partnership
- Pitcher Don Larsen throws a perfect game in World Series
- Oral vaccine for polio manufactured
- Dear Abbey answers her first letter
- First Black student to University of Alabama suspended
- In God We Trust motto authorized
- Martin Luther King Jr.'s home bombed
- Dove ice cream bar invented
- Sprinter Bobby Morrow wins 3 gold medals in 1956 Olympics
- Yahtzee goes on sale
- Robby the Robot appears
- Didrikson, voted greatest Female Athlete of the First Half of the 20th century, died
- "Does she… or doesn't she?" hair dye ad slogan coined

Born this year:
- Actress Carrie Fisher
- Actor Tom Hanks
- Illusionist David Copperfield

Library of Congress

Grace Kelly, aged 26 and retiring from acting, sets sail for Monaco and her impending wedding to Prince Rainier III. The wedding was watched live by more than 30 million people.

On the Bookshelf
When You Were Small

The books of our childhood linger long in the memory. These are the children's classics, all published in your first ten years. Do you remember the stories? What about the covers?

1956	The Hundred and One Dalmatians by Dodie Smith
1956	Old Yeller by Fred Gipson
1957	Little Bear by Else Holmelund Minarik
1957	The Cat in the Hat by Dr. Seuss
1958	The Witch of Blackbird Pond by Elizabeth George Speare
1958	The House That Jack Built by Antonio Frasconi
1959	The Rescuers by Margery Sharp
1959	My Side of the Mountain by Jean George
1960	Are You My Mother? by P.D. Eastman
1960	Green Eggs and Ham by Dr. Seuss
1961	James and the Giant Peach by Roald Dahl
1961	Go, Dog. Go! by P.D. Eastman
1961	The Bronze Bow by Elizabeth George Speare
1962	A Wrinkle in Time by Madeleine L'Engle
1962	**The Snowy Day by Ezra Jack Keats** The first award-winning children's book to feature an African-American protagonist. Keats—who was born Ezra Katz—grew up in tenement housing. This was his first solo project.
1962	Mr. Rabbit and the Lovely Present by Charlotte Zolotow
1963	Where the Wild Things Are by Maurice Sendak
1963	Clifford the Big Red Dog by Norman Bridwell
1964	**The Giving Tree by Shel Silverstein** Is this the most controversial apple tree in literature? The Giving Tree is a story of love and regularly ranks as a parental favorite. But for some it's a tale of taking selfishly, not giving—definitely one to be left on the shelf.
1964	Charlie and the Chocolate Factory by Roald Dahl
1964	**Chitty-Chitty-Bang-Bang by Ian Fleming** Published after Fleming's death, the book was adapted for film four years later, produced by Albert R. Broccoli and co-written by Roald Dahl.

Around the World in Your Birth Year

Here are the events from outside the US that were big enough to make news back home in the year you were born. And you won't remember any of them!

+ Khrushchev denounces Stalin
+ Eurovision song contest begins
+ Monaco's Rainier marries Grace Kelly
+ Soviet crush Hungarian rebellion
+ Suez Crisis begins
+ Gasoline rationing begins in UK
+ Tunisia becomes independent
+ Winter Olympics open in Italy
+ Olympics open in Melbourne
+ Canada imports Sony transistor radios
+ Fire damages Eiffel Tower
+ Egypt expels British troops
+ British jet sets air speed record
+ Morocco wins independence
+ Woman becomes mayor in Greece
+ Climbers ascend Lhotse
+ India opens diplomatic relations with Franco's Spain
+ Nasser becomes president of Egypt
+ Interpol is named
+ Polish workers protest, violently crushed by Soviets
+ West Germany bans the Communist Party
+ Pakistan becomes Islamic republic
+ Fidel Castro leads Cuban rebellion
+ Pele joins Brazilian team
+ Two ocean liners collide off the US coast

Boys' Names When You Were Born

Once upon a time, popular names came…
and stuck. (John hogged the top spot for 40
years, to 1924.) These are the most popular
names when you were born.

Michael
For 44 years from 1954 onwards, Michael was the nation's
most popular name. (There was one blip in 1960 when
David came first.)

James
Robert
David
John
William
Richard
Mark
Thomas
Steven
Charles
Joseph
Gary
Donald
Ronald
Kenneth
Paul
Daniel
Timothy
Jeffrey
Larry
Kevin
Stephen
Gregory
Edward
Dennis

Rising and falling stars:
Farewell Ernest; welcome Matthew and Dean; and congrats
to Randy who achieved his highest position of 28th.

Girls' Names When You Were Born

On the girls' side of the maternity ward, Mary held the crown in every year from 1880 to 1946—and she was back on top by 1953 for a further nine years.

Mary
Debra

Debra, or Deborah? Debra was usually the underdog but in 1956, she finally go the upper hand. Deborah regrouped, and five years later she was back on top.

Linda
Deborah
Susan
Patricia
Karen
Cynthia
Barbara
Donna
Nancy
Pamela
Sharon
Sandra
Diane
Carol
Kathleen
Cheryl
Brenda
Kathy
Janet
Elizabeth
Denise
Teresa
Margaret
Janice

Rising and falling stars:

No exits in 1956, but in come Kimberly, Tina, Dawn, Angela and Jennifer.

Things People Did When You Were Growing Up...

...that hardly anyone does now. Some of these we remember fondly; others are best left in the past!

- ✦ Help Mom make cookies using a cookie press
- ✦ Keep bread in a breadbox
- ✦ Can and preserve vegetables from your garden
- ✦ Listen to daytime soap operas on the radio
- ✦ Participate in Church fundraisers
- ✦ Watch endurance competitions like flagpole sitting and goldfish eating
- ✦ Build scooters from roller skates and scrap wood
- ✦ Bring a slide-rule to math class
- ✦ Take a Sunday drive out to the country
- ✦ Play leapfrog
- ✦ Live in a Sears Modern Home ordered from the Sears catalog
- ✦ Get a treat from the pharmacy soda fountain
- ✦ Camp in a "Hooverville" while looking for work
- ✦ Keep a thrift or kitchen garden
- ✦ Buy penny candy
- ✦ Buy goods from door-to-door salesmen
- ✦ Wear clothing made from flour sacks
- ✦ Collect marbles
- ✦ Join a dance marathon
- ✦ Listen to Amos n' Andy on the radio on weekend evenings
- ✦ Eat Water Pie
- ✦ "Window shop" downtown on Saturdays
- ✦ Pitch pennies
- ✦ Earn $30 a month plus food and shelter working for the Civilian Conservation Corps

How Many of These Games Are Still Played?

The first half of the 20th century was the heyday for new board and card games launched to the US public. Some are still firm family favorites, but which ones did you play when you were young?

1925	Pegity
1925	Playing for the Cup
1927	Hokum ("The game for a roomful")
1920s	The Greyhound Racing Game
1930	Wahoo
1932	Finance
1934	Sorry!
1935	**Monopoly** The game's origins lie with The Landlord's Game, patented in 1904 by Elizabeth Magie. (The anti-monopoly version—Prosperity—didn't catch on.) It was the first game with a never-ending path rather than a fixed start and finish.
1935	Easy Money
1936	The Amazing Adventures of Fibber McGee
1937	Meet the Missus
1937	Stock Ticker
1938	Scrabble
1938	Movie Millions
1940	Dig
1940	Prowl Car
1942	Sea Raider
1943	Chutes and Ladders
1949	**Clue** Clue—or Cluedo, as it is known to most outside the USA—introduced us to a host of shady characters and grisly murder weapons. For years those included a piece of genuine lead pipe, now replaced on health grounds.
1949	**Candy Land** This wholesome family racing game, invented on a polio ward, was the victim of something less savory nearly 50 years after its launch when an adult website claimed the domain name. Thankfully, the courts swiftly intervened.

Things People Do Now...

...that were virtually unknown when you were young.
How many of these habits are part of your routine or even
second nature these days? Do you remember the first time?

- ✦ Get curbside grocery pickup
- ✦ Stream movies instead of going to Blockbuster for a rental
- ✦ Learn remotely and online
- ✦ Communicate by text or video chat
- ✦ Use a Kindle or other e-reading device
- ✦ Go geocaching
- ✦ Track your sleep, exercise, or fertility with a watch
- ✦ Use a weighted blanket
- ✦ Use a robotic/automatic vacuum
- ✦ Take your dog to a dog park
- ✦ Have a package delivered by drone
- ✦ Find a date online or through an app
- ✦ Use hand sanitizer
- ✦ Automatically soothe your baby with a self-rocking bassinet
- ✦ Host a gender-reveal party during pregnancy
- ✦ Use a home essential oil diffuser or salt lamp
- ✦ Have a "destination wedding"
- ✦ Use a device charging station while waiting for a flight
- ✦ Get a ride from Uber or Lyft instead of a taxi
- ✦ Drink hard seltzer
- ✦ Take a home DNA test (for you... or your pet)
- ✦ Have a telemedicine/virtual healthcare visit
- ✦ Smoke an e-cigarette/"vape"
- ✦ Start your car, dryer, or air conditioner via an app

Popular Food in the 1950s

For many, the post-war years meant more of one thing in particular on the table: meat. In the yard, men stepped up to the barbeque to sharpen their skills. In the kitchen, fancy new electric appliances and frozen TV dinners promised convenience and new, exotic flavors.

Tuna noodle casserole
Dinty Moore Beef Stew
Beef stroganoff

Green bean casserole
Green bean casserole was invented in the Campbell's test kitchen in 1955 as a cheap, fuss-free dish. Today, around 40 percent of Campbell's Cream of Mushroom soup sold in the US goes into this dinner table staple.

Pigs-in-a-blanket
Pigs get different blankets in the United Kingdom, where sausages are wrapped in bacon rather than pastry.

Backyard barbecues
Ovaltine
Swedish meatballs
Pineapple upside down cake

Spam
Ground pork shoulder and ham sold in a distinctive can—for much of the world, that means Spam. This "meatloaf without basic training" is affordable and still popular, with over eight billion cans sold since it was first sold in 1937.

Ambrosia salad
Sugar Smacks
Cheez Whiz
Stuffed celery
Campbell's Tomato Soup spice cake

Swanson Turkey TV Dinners
Dreamed up as a solution to an over-supply of turkey, TV dinners proved nearly as popular as the TV itself. Swanson sold over 25 million of them in 1954, the year these handy meal packs were launched.

Veg-All canned vegetables
Chicken à la King

Cars of the 1950s

Was this the golden age of automobiles? In truth, some of these models had been brought to market long before, such as the Buick Roadmaster and the Studebaker Champion. But even stalwarts were quick to adopt the Space Age theme of the decade as sweeping lines, tailfins, and cascading chrome grilles became the norm.

1926	Chrysler Imperial
1936	General Motors Buick Roadmaster
1939	**Studebaker Champion**

Over seven decades, the Champion's creator, Raymond Loewy, designed railroads, logos, buses, vending machines, and a space station for NASA.

1939	Chrysler DeSoto Custom
1947	Studebaker Starlight Coupe
1948	**Crosley Station Wagon**

The first car to be marketed as "Sports Utility."

1948	Jaguar XK120
1949	**Muntz Jet**

Fewer than 200 Muntz Jets were built by founder Madman Muntz, an engineer who married seven times and made (and lost) fortunes selling cars, TVs, and more.

1949	Chrysler Dodge Coronet
1950	General Motors Chevrolet Bel-Air
1950	Nash Rambler
1951	Hudson Hornet
1953	General Motors Chevrolet Corvette
1953	General Motors Buick Skylark
1953	General Motors Cadillac Eldorado
1953	Nash Metropolitan
1954	Ford Skyliner
1955	Ford Thunderbird
1955	Ford Fairlane
1956	Studebaker Golden Hawk
1956	Chrysler Plymouth Fury
1957	**Mercedes-Benz 300 SL Roadster**

Voted "Sports Car of the Century" in 1999.

Cars crawl out of 1950s Philadelphia over the Ben Franklin Bridge. Henry Ford wasn't the only one to "build a car for the great multitude." Millions of new suburbanites embraced their newfound freedom— even if that meant driving to the same place as everyone else.

The Biggest Hits When You Were 10

Whistled by your father, hummed by your sister or overheard on the radio, these are the hit records as you reached double digits.

The Troggs 🎵 Wild Thing
Nancy Sinatra 🎵 These Boots Are Made for Walkin'
Frank Sinatra 🎵 Strangers in the Night
The Beatles 🎵 Eleanor Rigby
Percy Sledge 🎵 When a Man Loves a Woman
The Mamas and the Papas 🎵 California Dreamin'
Simon and Garfunkel 🎵 The Sound of Silence
The Young Rascals 🎵 Good Lovin'
The Mindbenders 🎵 A Groovy Kind of Love
The Beatles 🎵 We Can Work It Out
The Four Tops 🎵 Reach Out (I'll Be There)
The Monkees 🎵 Last Train to Clarksville
The Lovin' Spoonful 🎵 Summer in the City
Buck Owens 🎵 Think of Me
The Supremes 🎵 You Can't Hurry Love
Donovan 🎵 Mellow Yellow
Loretta Lynn 🎵 Dear Uncle Sam
The Association 🎵 Cherish
The Rolling Stones 🎵 Paint It Black
Johnny Rivers 🎵 Poor Side of Town
Sonny James 🎵 Take Good Care of Her
The Rolling Stones 🎵 Mother's Little Helper
Wilson Pickett 🎵 Mustang Sally
Ike and Tina Turner 🎵 River Deep, Mountain High

Faster, Easier, Better

Yesterday's technological breakthrough is today's modern convenience. Here are some of the lab and engineering marvels that were made before you turned 21 years old.

1956	Hard Disk Drive
1956	Operating system (OS)
1957	Laser
1958	Microchip
1959	Weather satellite
1960	Global navigation satellite system
1961	Spreadsheet (electronic)
1962	Red LED

1963 **Computer mouse**
The inventor of the computer mouse had patented it in 1963. However, by the time the mouse became commercially available in the 1980s, his patent had expired. The first computer system that made use of a (giant) mouse came from Xerox in 1981.

1964	Plasma display
1965	Hypertext (http)
1966	Computer RAM
1967	Hand-held calculator
1968	Virtual Reality
1969	Laser printer

1970 **Wireless local area network**
The first wireless local network was developed by the University of Hawaii to communicate data among the Hawaiian Islands.

1971	Email
1972	Video games console (Magnavox Odyssey)
1973	Mobile phone
1974	Universal Product Code (barcode)
1975	Ethernet
1976	Apple Computer

Across the Nation

Double digits at last: you're old enough to eavesdrop on adults and scan the headlines. These may be some of the earliest national news stories you remember.

- Kevlar invented
- John Lennon's "Jesus" comment sparks outrage
- Uniform Time Act signed
- Supreme Court decides Miranda v. Arizona
- National Organization for Women founded
- Richard Speck murders eight nurses
- Charles Whitman commits murder from atop UT tower
- Caesars Palace opens in Las Vegas
- Actor Ronald Reagan elected governor of California
- First Kwanzaa celebrated
- Department of Transportation established
- Quaker Instant Oatmeal introduced
- NASA completes several Gemini missions
- Draft Deferment Test given
- Race riots across Atlanta and other US cities
- First black member of President's cabinet appointed (Robert C. Weaver)
- Pro football game with the highest score ever played
- Artificial heart implanted
- Grenada school segregation protests
- Medicare takes effect
- Walt Disney died
- Billie Jean King wins Wimbledon
- The Met moves to the Lincoln Center
- Two national football leagues to merge into one entity

Born this year:
- Singer Janet Jackson
- Actor David Schwimmer
- Model Cindy Crawford

Kapow! Comic Books and Heroes from Your Childhood

Barely a year went past in the mid-20th Century without a new super-powered hero arriving to save the day. Here are some that were taking on the bad guys during your childhood.

G.I. Combat ✻ The Haunted Tank

Donald Duck ✻ Donald Duck

Fantastic Four ✻ The Thing

Tales To Astonish ✻ Ant-Man

Uncle Scrooge ✻ Uncle Scrooge

The Incredible Hulk ✻ Hulk

The Avengers ✻ Thor

Action Comics ✻ Superman

Wonder Woman ✻ Wonder Woman

The Amazing Spider-Man ✻ Spider-Man

Detective Comics ✻ Batman

Daredevil ✻ Daredevil

The X-Men ✻ X-Men

Tales of Suspense ✻ Captain America

Sgt. Fury & His
Howling Commandos ✻ **Nick Fury**
The title was chosen as a bet: co-creator Stan Lee reckoned that he and Jack Kirby could find success with a silly name—and they did just that.

Strange Tales ✻ Doctor Strange

Showcase ✻ The Spectre

Iron Man ✻ Iron Man

The Phantom Stranger ✻ The Phantom Stranger

The Flash ✻ Wally West

Green Lantern ✻ Hal Jordan

Adventure Comics ✻ Supergirl

Winners of the Stanley Cup Since You Were Born

The prestigious Stanley Cup has been changing hands since 1893, although the trophy itself has been redesigned more than once. Here are the teams to lift the champagne-filled cup since you were born.

- Detroit Red Wings (4)
- Chicago Black Hawks (4)
- **Boston Bruins (3)**
  1970: Bobby Orr scored perhaps the most famous goal in NHL history, in midair, to clinch the title.
- **New York Rangers (1)**
  After a 1940 victory, the Rangers would not win another Stanley Cup for another 54 years.
- Toronto Maple Leafs (4)
- Montreal Canadiens (17)
- Philadelphia Flyers (2)
- New York Islanders (4)
- Edmonton Oilers (5)
- **Calgary Flames (1)**
  1989 was the last time a Stanley Cup Final has been played between two teams from Canada.
- Pittsburgh Penguins (5)
- New Jersey Devils (3)
- **Colorado Avalanche (2)**
  1996: A win in their first season after moving from Quebec (where their nickname was the Nordiques).
- Dallas Stars (1)
- Tampa Bay Lightning (3)
- Carolina Hurricanes (1)
- Anaheim Ducks (1)
- Los Angeles Kings (2)
- Washington Capitals (1)
- St. Louis Blues (1)

On the Silver Screen When You Were 11

From family favorites to the films you weren't allowed to watch, these are the films and actors that drew the praise and the crowds when you turned 11.

El Dorado 🎬 John Wayne, Robert Mitchum, James Caan

The Jungle Book 🎬 Phil Harris, Sebastian Cabot, George Sanders
The Beatles were planned to appear, but John Lennon refused to work on animated films.

In the Heat of the Night 🎬 Sidney Poitier, Rod Steiger, Lee Grant

Valley of the Dolls 🎬 Barbara Parkins, Patty Duke, Sharon Tate

In Like Flint 🎬 James Coburn, Lee J. Cobb, Jerry Goldsmith

Divorce American Style 🎬 Dick Van Dyke, Debbie Reynolds, Jason Robards

Guess Who's Coming to Dinner 🎬 Spencer Tracy, Sidney Poitier, Katharine Hepburn

The Born Losers 🎬 Tom Laughlin, Elizabeth James, Jeremy Slate

Doctor Dolittle 🎬 Rex Harrison, Samantha Eggar, Anthony Newley

Dirty Dozen 🎬 Lee Marvin, Ernest Borgnine, Jim Brown

The Graduate 🎬 Dustin Hoffman, Anne Bancroft, Katharine Ross

The War Wagon 🎬 John Wayne, Kirk Douglas, Howard Keel

The Taming of the Shrew 🎬 Elizabeth Taylor, Richard Burton, Natasha Pyne

In Cold Blood 🎬 Robert Blake, Scott Wilson, John Forsythe

Hombre 🎬 Paul Newman, Frederic March, Richard Boone

Thoroughly Modern Millie 🎬 Julie Andrews, Mary Tyler Moore, James Fox

Wait Until Dark 🎬 Audrey Hepburn, Alan Arkin, Richard Crenna

Casino Royale 🎬 Peter Sellers, Ursula Andress, Barbara Bouchet

Camelot 🎬 Richard Harris, Vanessa Redgrave, Franco Nero

The Ambushers 🎬 Dean Martin, Senta Berger, Janice Rule

Cool Hand Luke 🎬 Paul Newman, George Kennedy, J.D. Cannon

Bonnie and Clyde 🎬 Warren Beatty, Faye Dunaway

To Sir With Love 🎬 Sidney Poitier, Christian Roberts, Judy Geeson
The film's title song was the best-selling single in the United States in 1967.

You Only Live Twice 🎬 Sean Connery, Akiko Wakabayashi, Mie Hama

Comic Strips You'll Know

Comic strips took off in the late 19th century and for much of the 20th century they were a dependable feature of everyday life. Some were solo efforts; others became so-called zombie strips, living on well beyond their creator. A century on, some are still going. But how many from your youth will you remember?

1940–52	The Spirit by Will Eisner
1930–	**Blondie** In 1995, Blondie was one of 20 strips commemorated by the US Postal Service in the Comic Strip Classics series.
1931–	**Dick Tracy** Gould's first idea? A detective called Plainclothes Tracy.
1930–95	Mickey Mouse
1932–	Mary Worth
1936–	**The Phantom** Lee Falk worked on The Phantom for 63 years and Mandrake The Magician for 65.
1919–	Barney Google and Snuffy Smith
1938–	Nancy
1946–	Mark Trail
1937–	**Prince Valiant** Edward, the Duke of Windsor (previously Edward VIII), called Prince Valiant the "greatest contribution to English literature in the past hundred years."
1934–2003	**Flash Gordon** Alex Raymond created Flash Gordon to compete with the Buck Rogers comic strip.
1934–77	Li'l Abner by Al Capp
1925–74	Etta Kett by Paul Robinson
1947–69	Grandma by Charles Kuhn
1948–	Rex Morgan, M.D.
1933–87	Brick Bradford
1950–2000	**Peanuts by Charles M. Schulz** Schultz was inducted into the Hockey Hall of Fame after building the Redwood Empire Arena near his studio.
1950–	Beetle Bailey

Biggest Hits by The King

He may have conquered rock'n'roll, but Elvis's success straddled genres including country music, R&B, and more. These are his Number 1s from across the charts, beginning with the rockabilly "I Forgot..." through the posthumous country hit, "Guitar Man."

I Forgot to Remember to Forget (1955)
Heartbreak Hotel (1956)
I Want You, I Need You, I Love You (1956)
Don't Be Cruel (1956)
Hound Dog (1956)
Love Me Tender (1956)
Too Much (1957)
All Shook Up (1957)
(Let Me Be Your) Teddy Bear (1957)
Jailhouse Rock (1957)
Don't (1957)
Wear My Ring Around Your Neck (1958)
Hard Headed Woman (1958)
A Big Hunk O' Love (1959)
Stuck On You (1960)
It's Now or Never (1960)
Are You Lonesome Tonight? (1960)
Surrender (1961)
Good Luck Charm (1962)
Suspicious Minds (1969)
Moody Blue (1976)
Way Down (1977)
Guitar Man (1981)

Childhood Candies

In labs across the country, mid-century food scientists dreamed up new and colorful ways to delight children just like you. These are the fruits of their labor, launched before you turned twenty-one.

1950s	Swedish Fish (Malaco)
1950s	Look! Candy Bar (Golden Nugget Candy Co.)
1960	Sixlets (Leaf Brands)
1962	Now and Later (Phoenix Candy Company)
1962	**SweeTarts** (Sunline, Inc.) These have the same candy base as Pixy Stix which was invented using drink powder from a children's drink.
1962	LemonHead (Ferrara Candy Company)
1963	**Cadbury Creme Eggs** (Fry's) An original 1963 Fry's Creme Egg (as they were then called) was discovered in 2017. It hasn't been eaten.
1964	100 Grand Bar (Nestle)
1960s	Spree (Sunline Candy Company)
1966	Razzles (Fleer)
1967	**M&M Fruit Chewies** (Mars) In 1960, Mars launched "Opal Fruits" in the UK, possibly after a competition entry from a boy named Peter. Seven years later, they appeared in the US as Starburst. It took 20 years for the name to be standardized worldwide.
1968	Caramello Bar (Cadbury)
1971	Laffy Taffy (Beich's)
1971	Snickers Munch Bar (Mars)
1972	Bottle Caps (Nestle/Willy Wonka)
1973	**Marathon Bar** (Mars) Eight inches of chocolate-covered caramel, Marathon was only sold for 8 short years. You can still buy it in the UK, where it's called a Curly-Wurly...and what was once sold as a Marathon is now Snickers.

Books of the Decade

Ten years of your life that took you from adventure books aged 10 to dense works of profundity at 20—or perhaps just grown-up adventures! How many did you read when they were first published?

1966	Valley of the Dolls by Jacqueline Susann
1966	In Cold Blood by Truman Capote
1967	Rosemary's Baby by Ira Levin
1967	The Arrangement by Elia Kazan
1967	The Confessions of Nat Turner by William Styron
1968	Airport by Arthur Hailey
1968	Couples by John Updike
1969	The Godfather by Mario Puzo
1969	Slaughterhouse-Five by Kurt Vonnegut
1969	Portnoy's Complaint by Philip Roth
1969	The French Lieutenant's Woman by John Fowles
1970	Love Story by Erich Segal
1970	One Hundred Years of Solitude by Gabriel Garcia Marquez
1971	The Happy Hooker: My Own Story by Xaviera Hollander
1971	The Exorcist by William Peter Blatty
1972	Watership Down by Richard Adams
1972	The Joy of Sex by Alex Comfort
1972	Fear and Loathing in Las Vegas by Hunter S. Thompson
1973	Fear of Flying by Erica Jong
1973	Gravity's Rainbow by Thomas Pynchon
1974	Jaws by Peter Benchley
1974	The Front Runner by Patricia Nell Warren
1975	The Eagle Has Landed by Jack Higgins
1975	Shōgun by James Clavell
1975	Ragtime by E.L. Doctorow

US Buildings

Some were loathed then, loved now; others, the reverse. Some broke new architectural ground; others housed famous or infamous businesses, or helped to power a nation. All of them were built in your first 18 years.

1956	**Capitol Records Building, Los Angeles** The world's first circular office building.
1957	666 Fifth Avenue, New York City
1958	Time & Life Building, New York City
1959	2 Broadway, New York City
1960	Four Gateway Center, Pittsburgh
1961	One Chase Manhattan Plaza
1962	Kennedy Space Center, Florida
1963	**MetLife Building, New York City** The largest office space in the world when it opened, the MetLife was born as the Pan Am Building, complete with heliport and 15 ft. lit signage atop (the last permitted).
1964	277 Park Avenue, New Yor City
1965	Cheyenne Mountain complex, Colorado
1966	John F. Kennedy Federal Building, Boston
1967	Watergate Hotel and Office Complex
1968	**John Hancock Center, Chicago** Second-highest in the world when it opened, the tower is still a creditable 33rd tallest when measured to the tip of its antenna.
1969	Transamerica Pyramid, San Francisco
1970	World Trade Center Twin Towers
1971	Blue Cross Blue Shield of Michigan, Detroit
1972	One Astor Plaza, New York City
1973	**Sears Tower (now Willis Tower), Chicago** Sears Tower was the world's tallest building for nearly a quarter of a century. It was first climbed (on the outside) in 1981.
1974	New York Merchandise Mart

Radio DJs from Your Childhood

If the radio was the soundtrack to your life as you grew up, some of these voices were part of the family. (The stations listed are where these DJs made their name; the dates are their radio broadcasting career).

Wolfman Jack 🎙 XERB/Armed Forces Radio (1960–1995)
Jocko Henderson 🎙 WDAS/W LIB (1952–1991)
Casey Kasem 🎙 KRLA (1954–2010)
Kasem was the host of American Top 40 for four decades. By 1986, his show was broadcast on 1,000 radio stations.

Bruce Morrow 🎙 WABC (1959–)
Murray Kaufman 🎙 WINS (1958–1975)
You'll likely remember him as Murray the K, the self-declared "fifth Beatle" (he played a lot of music from the Fab Four).

Alison Steele 🎙 WNEW-FM (1966–1995)
Aka The Nightbird, Steele was that rarity of the sixties and seventies: a successful female DJ.

Alan Freed 🎙 WJW/WINS (1945–1965)
Freed's career crashed after he was found to have been taking payola. His contribution was recognized posthumously when admitted into the Rock n Roll Hall of Fame.

Robert W. Morgan 🎙 KHJ-AM (1955–1998)
Dan Ingram 🎙 WABC (1958–2004)
Dave Hull 🎙 KRLA (1955–2010)
Another candidate for the "fifth Beatle," Hull interviewed the band many times.

Hal Jackson 🎙 WBLS (1940–2011)
Johnny Holliday 🎙 KYA (1956–)
Herb Kent 🎙 WVON (1944–2016)
"Cool Gent" Herb Kent was the longest-serving DJ on the radio.

Tom Donahue 🎙 WIBG/KYA (1949–1975)
John R. 🎙 WLAC (1941–1973)
Bill Randle 🎙 WERE/WCBS (1940s–2004)
Jack Spector 🎙 WMCA (1955–1994)
Spector, one of WMCA's "Good Guys," died on air in 1994. A long silence after playing "I'm in the Mood for Love" alerted station staff.

It Happened in 1972

Here's a round-up of the most newsworthy events from across the US in the year you turned (sweet) 16.

- Nixon wins re-election
- The world's greatest jewel heist? Eight rob the Pierre Hotel
- Dallas Cowboys win the Super Bowl
- Shirley Chisholm announces her run for president
- Bob Douglas elected to Basketball Hall of Fame
- Equal Rights Amendment passes
- President Nixon visits China
- Coal sludge spill kills over 125
- Gov. George Wallace shot while campaigning for presidency
- Watergate burglars arrested
- Black Hills Flood strikes
- Hurricane Agnes hits the East Coast
- No new draftees to Vietnam announced
- Supreme Court rules death penalty unconstitutional
- Actress Jane Fonda tours Vietnam
- Health officials admit to Tuskegee study scandal
- Swimmer Mark Spitz wins 7 Olympic gold medals (right)
- Riot breaks out on USS Kitty Hawk
- FBI hires first female agents
- HBO begins as subscription cable-provider service
- Apollo 17 returns safely
- Football's "Immaculate Reception" completed
- Women run the Boston Marathon
- Black Lung Benefit bill signed

Born this year:
- Rapper Eminem
- Actress Cameron Diaz
- Actor Ben Affleck

Seven events, seven gold medals, seven world records: Mark Spitz's performance at the 1972 Munich Olympics was unprecedented. It was another 36 years before his achievement was surpassed when Michael Phelps won 8 gold medals in Beijing.

News Anchors of the Fifties and Sixties

Trusted, familiar, and exclusively male: these are the faces that brought you the news, and the catchphrases they made their own.

Edward R. Murrow 📺 CBS (1938-59)
"Good night, and good luck."

Walter Cronkite 📺 CBS (1962-81)
"And that's the way it is."

David Brinkley 📺 NBC (1956-71)
"Good night, Chet..."

Chet Huntley 📺 NBC (1956-70)
"...Good night, David."

Harry Reasoner 📺 CBS & ABC (1961-91)

Frank Reynolds 📺 ABC (1968-70)

John Charles Daly 📺 CBS & ABC (1941-60)
"Good night and a good tomorrow."

Douglas Edwards 📺 CBS (1948-62)

Hugh Downs 📺 NBC (1962-71)

John Chancellor 📺 NBC (1970-82)

Paul Harvey 📺 ABC Radio (1951-2009)
"Hello Americans, this is Paul Harvey. Stand by for news!"

Mike Wallace 📺 CBS (1963-66)

John Cameron Swayze 📺 NBC (1948-56)
"Well, that's the story, folks! This is John Cameron Swayze, and I'm glad we could get together."

Ron Cochran 📺 ABC (1962-65)

Bob Young 📺 ABC (1967-68)

Dave Garroway 📺 NBC (1952-61)

Bill Shadel 📺 ABC (1960-63)

Fifties Game Shows

It all started so well: appointment radio became appointment TV, with new and crossover game shows bringing us together. But as the decade progressed, the scandal emerged: some shows were fixed. Quiz shows were down, but certainly not out. (Dates include periods off-air.)

Break the Bank 🏆 (1945–57)

Beat The Clock 🏆 (1950–2019)

Name That Tune 🏆 (1952–85)
A radio crossover that spawned 25 international versions.

Strike It Rich 🏆 (1947–58)

The Price Is Right 🏆 (1956–65)
The original version of the current quiz that began in 1972. This one was hosted by Bill Cullen.

Down You Go 🏆 (1951–56)

I've Got A Secret 🏆 (1952–2006)

What's The Story 🏆 (1951–55)

The $64,000 Question 🏆 (1955–58)

People Are Funny 🏆 (1942–60)

Tic-Tac-Dough 🏆 (1956–90)
Early Tic-Tac-Dough contestants were often coached; around three-quarters of the shows in one run were rigged.

The Name's The Same 🏆 (1951–55)

Two For The Money 🏆 (1952–57)

The Big Payoff 🏆 (1951–62)

Twenty-One 🏆 (1956–58)
At the heart of the rigging scandal, Twenty-One was the subject of Robert Redford's 1994 movie, Quiz Show.

Masquerade Party 🏆 (1952–60)

You Bet Your Life 🏆 (1947–61)
A comedy quiz hosted by Groucho Marx.

Truth or Consequences 🏆 (1940–88)
Started life as a radio quiz. TV host Bob Barker signed off with: "Hoping all your consequences are happy ones."

20 Questions 🏆 (1946–55)

What's My Line 🏆 (1950–75)

Liberty Issue Stamps

First released in 1954, the Liberty Issue drew its name from not one but three depictions of the Statue of Liberty across the denominations. (There was only room for one "real" woman, though.) It coincided with the new era of stamp collecting as a childhood hobby that endured for decades. Were you one of these new miniature philatelists?

Benjamin Franklin ½ ¢ Polymath (writer, inventor, scientist)
Franklin discovered the principle of electricity,
the Law of Conservation of Charge.

George Washington 1 ¢ First US President
Palace of the Governors 1 ¼ ¢
A building in Santa Fe, New Mexico that served as
the seat of government of New Mexico for centuries.

Mount Vernon 1 ½ ¢ George Washington's plantation
Thomas Jefferson 2 ¢ Polymath; third US President
Bunker Hill Monument 2 ½ ¢ Battle site of the Revolutionary War
Statue of Liberty 3 ¢ Gifted by the people of France
Abraham Lincoln 4 ¢ 16th US President
Lincoln received a patent for a flotation device that assisted
boats in moving through shallow water.

The Hermitage 4 ½ ¢ Andrew Jackson's plantation
James Monroe 5 ¢ Fifth US President
Theodore Roosevelt 6 ¢ 26th US President
Woodrow Wilson 7 ¢ 28th US President; served during WW1
John J. Pershing 8 ¢ US Army officer during World War I
Alamo 9 ¢ Site of a pivotal Texas Revolution battle
Independence Hall 10 ¢ Independence declared here
Benjamin Harrison 12 ¢ 23rd US President
John Jay 15 ¢ First Chief Justice of the United States
Monticello 20 ¢ Thomas Jefferson's plantation
Paul Revere 25 ¢ Alerted militia of the British approach
Robert E. Lee 30 ¢ Confederate general in the Civil War
John Marshall 40 ¢ Fourth Chief Justice of the US
Susan B. Anthony 50 ¢ Women's suffrage activist
Patrick Henry $1 Leader of the Dec. of Independence
Alexander Hamilton $5 First Secretary of the Treasury

The Biggest Hits When You Were 16

The artists that topped the charts when you turned 16 might not be in your top 10 these days, but you'll probably remember them!

Don McLean ♪ American Pie
Chicago ♪ Saturday in the Park
3 Dog Night ♪ Never Been to Spain
Neil Young ♪ Heart of Gold
Harry Nilsson ♪ Without You
Hot Butter ♪ Popcorn
Bill Withers ♪ Lean on Me
Jerry Lee Lewis ♪ Chantilly Lace
Sammy Davis Jr. ♪ The Candyman
Cat Stevens ♪ Morning Has Broken
Looking Glass ♪ Brandy (You're a Fine Girl)
John Fogerty
and the Blue Ridge Rangers ♪ Jambalaya (On the Bayou)
Billy Paul ♪ Me and Mrs. Jones
Donna Fargo ♪ The Happiest Girl in the Whole USA
Stevie Wonder ♪ Superstition
Elton John ♪ Crocodile Rock
The Main Ingredient ♪ Everybody Plays the Fool
Faron Young ♪ It's Four in the Morning
The Moody Blues ♪ Nights in White Satin
Harold Melvin
and the Blue Notes ♪ If You Don't Know Me by Now
Roberta Flack ♪ The First Time Ever I Saw Your Face
The Staple Singers ♪ I'll Take You There
Gilbert O'Sullivan ♪ Alone Again (Naturally)
Dr. Hook and
the Medicine Show ♪ The Cover of the Rolling Stone

Medical Advances Before You Were 21

A baby born in 1920 USA had a life expectancy of just 55.4 years. By 2000 that was up to 76.8, thanks to medical advances including many of these.

1956	**Metered-dose inhaler** Invented after the teen daughter of head of Riker Labs asked why her asthma medicine couldn't be in a can like hair spray. At the time, asthma medicine was given in ineffective squeeze bulb glass containers.
1958	Pacemaker
1959	Bone marrow transplant
1959	In vitro fertilization
1960	CPR
1960	The pill
1960	Coronary artery bypass surgery
1962	Hip replacement
1962	Beta blocker
1962	First oral polio vaccine (Sabin)
1963	Liver and lung transplants
1963	Valium
1963	Artificial heart
1964	Measles vaccine
1965	Portable defibrillator
1966	Pancreas transplant
1967	Mumps vaccine
1967	Heart transplant
1968	Powered prosthesis
1968	Controlled drug delivery
1969	Cochlear implant
1971	CAT scan
1972	Insulin pump
1973	MRI Scanning
1973	Laser eye surgery (LASIK)
1974	Liposuction
1976	First commercial PET scanner

Blockbuster Movies When You Were 16

These are the movies that everyone was talking about. How many of them did you see (or have you seen since)?

Joe Kidd 📽 Clint Eastwood, Robert Duvall, John Saxon

Lady Sings the Blues 📽 Diana Ross, Billy Dee Williams, Richard Pryor

Sounder 📽 Cicely Tyson, Paul Winfield, Kevin Hooks

The Last House on the Left 📽 Sandra Peabody, Lucy Grantham, David A. Hess

Tokyo Story 📽 Chishu Ryu, Chieko Higashiyama, Setsuko Hara

Shaft's Big Score 📽 Richard Roundtree, Moses Gunn

Across 110th Street 📽 Yaphet Kotto, Anthony Quinn, Anthony Franciosa
Anthony Quinn had wanted Sidney Poitier to play Lt. Pope.

The Valachi Papers 📽 Charles Bronson, Lino Ventura, Jill Ireland

Last Tango in Paris 📽 Marlon Brando, Maria Schneider, Maria Michi

Deep Throat 📽 Linda Lovelace, Harry Reems, Dolly Sharp

The Life and Times of Judge Roy Bean 📽 Paul Newman, Jacqueline Bisset, Anthony Perkins

Pete 'n' Tillie 📽 Walter Matthau, Carol Burnett, Geraldine Page

Frenzy 📽 Jon Finch, Alec McCowen, Barry Foster

Everything You Always Wanted to Know About Sex 📽 Woody Allen, John Carradine, Lou Jacobi

The Cowboys 📽 John Wayne, Roscoe Lee Browne, Slim Pickens

What's Up, Doc? 📽 Barbra Streisand, Ryan O'Neal, Kenneth Mars

Cabaret 📽 Liza Minnelli, Michael York, Joel Grey

Deliverance 📽 Jon Voight, Ned Beatty, Ronny Cox

Banshun 📽 Chishu Ryu, Setsuko Hara, Haruko Sugimura

The Godfather 📽 Marlon Brando, Al Pacino, James Caan

Conquest of the Planet of the Apes 📽 Roddy McDowall, Don Murray, Ricardo Montalban

The Poseidon Adventure 📽 Gene Hackman, Ernest Borgnine, Red Buttons

The Getaway 📽 Steve McQueen, Ali MacGraw, Ben Johnson

Jeremiah Johnson 📽 Robert Redford, Will Geer, Allyn Ann McLerie

Game Show Hosts of the Fifties and Sixties

Many of these men were semi-permanent fixtures, their voices and catchphrases ringing through the decades. Some were full-time entertainers; others were on sabbatical from more serious news duties.

John Charles Daly ►◄ What's My Line (1950–67)

Art Linkletter ►◄ People Are Funny (1943–60)

Garry Moore ►◄ I've Got A Secret (1956–64)

Groucho Marx ►◄ You Bet Your Life (1949–61)

Warren Hull ►◄ Strike It Rich (1947–58)

Herb Shriner ►◄ Two For The Money (1952–56)

George DeWitt ►◄ Name That Tune (1953–59)

Robert Q. Lewis ►◄ Name's The Same (1951–54)

Bill Cullen ►◄ The Price Is Right (1956–65)

Walter Cronkite ►◄ It's News To Me (1954)
"The most trusted man in America" was briefly the host of this topical quiz game. He didn't do it again.

Bill Slater ►◄ 20 Questions (1949–52)

Walter Kiernan ►◄ Who Said That (1951–54)

Bob Eubanks ►◄ The Newlywed Game (1966–74)

Bud Collyer ►◄ To Tell The Truth (1956–69)

Jack Barry ►◄ Twenty-One (1956–58)

Bert Parks ►◄ Break The Bank (1945–57)

Hugh Downs ►◄ Concentration (1958–69)

Mike Stokey ►◄ Pantomime Quiz (1947–59)

Allen Ludden ►◄ Password (1961–75)

Bob Barker ►◄ Truth or Consequences (1956–74)
Barker also spent 35 years hosting The Price Is Right.

Hal March ►◄ $64,000 Question (1955–58)

Monty Hall ►◄ Let's Make A Deal (1963–91)
Monty—born "Monte", but misspelled on an early publicity photo—was also a philanthropist who raised around $1 billion over his lifetime.

Johnny Carson ►◄ Who Do You Trust? (1957–63)

Kitchen Inventions

The 20th-century kitchen was a playground for food scientists and engineers with new labor-saving devices and culinary shortcuts launched every year. These all made their debut before you were 18.

1956	Saran wrap
1957	Homemaker tableware
1958	Rice-a-Roni
1959	Chocolate Velvet Cake invented
1960	**Automated dishwasher**

Electric dishwashers debuted in 1929 but to little acclaim, due in part to the Great Depression and WWII. Automated models with a drying element finally became popular in the 1970s.

1961	Mrs. Butterworth's syrup
1962	Chimney starter
1963	**Veg-O-Matic**

The Veg-O-Matic has increased the cultural lexicon in a number of ways, including "As Seen On TV" and "It slices and dices."

1964	Pop Tarts
1965	Bounty paper towels
1966	Cool Whip
1967	Countertop microwave
1968	Hunt snack pack
1969	Manwich
1970	Hamburger Helper
1971	**Crock Pot**

The hit show "This is Us" featured a tragic house fire caused directly by a defective Crock Pot. The company released an ad campaign to diffuse the publicity.

1972	Mr. Coffee
1973	Dawn dishwashing soap

Around the World When You Turned 18

These are the headlines from around the globe as you were catapulted into adulthood.

✦ Sextuplets born in Capetown
✦ IRA increases bombings in London
✦ Fire in Sao Paulo high rise kills 177, injures hundreds more
✦ Charles De Gaulle airport opens
✦ Soviet Union launches Salyut-4 space station
✦ Soccer stampede in Cairo kills 49
✦ Australia's Brisbane River floods
✦ Cyclone Tracy destroys the city of Darwin
✦ Smallpox epidemic strikes India
✦ Terracotta army found in China
✦ West Germany wins World Cup
✦ Golan Heights ceasefire is signed
✦ India tests nuclear weapon
✦ Lucy's bones found in Africa
✦ Turkey invades Cyprus
✦ All-female Japanese climbers ascend Manaslu
✦ Famine devastates several African nations
✦ French president dies while in office
✦ ABBA wins Eurovision
✦ Four car bombs kill over 40 in Ireland
✦ Ethiopian Civil War begins
✦ Portugal government overthrown by coup
✦ Argentina elects woman president
✦ Soviets revoke Alexander Solzhenitsyn's citizenship
✦ Deadly air crash in Paris kills 398

Super Bowl Champions Since You Were Born

These are the teams that have held a 7-pound, sterling silver Vince Lombardi trophy aloft during the Super Bowl era, and the number of times they've done it in your lifetime.

- **New England Patriots (6)**
  2001: The Super Bowl MVP, Tom Brady, had been a 6th round draft pick in 2000.
- Pittsburgh Steelers (6)
- Dallas Cowboys (5)
- San Francisco 49ers (5)
- **Green Bay Packers (4)**
  1967: To gain a berth in the Super Bowl, the Packers defeated the Dallas Cowboys in The Ice Bowl at 15 degrees below zero.
- New York Giants (4)
- **Denver Broncos (3)**
  2015: After the Broncos won their first Super Bowl 18 years prior, Broncos owner Pat Bowlen dedicated the victory to long-time quarterback John Elway ("This one's for John!"). After the 2015 victory, John Elway (now general manager) dedicated it to the ailing Bowlen ("This one's for Pat!").
- Washington Football Team (3)
- Las Vegas Raiders (3)
- Miami Dolphins (2)
- Indianapolis Colts (2)
- Kansas City Chiefs (2)
- Baltimore Ravens (2)
- Tampa Bay Buccaneers (2)
- **Los Angeles Rams (1)**
  1999: The Rams were led to the Super Bowl by Kurt Warner, who had been a grocery store clerk after college.
- Seattle Seahawks (1)
- Philadelphia Eagles (1)
- **Chicago Bears (1)**
  The 1985 Bears are known for their song, The Super Bowl Shuffle.
- New York Jets (1)
- New Orleans Saints (1)

Across the Nation

Voting. Joining the military. Turning 18 is serious stuff. Here's what everyone was reading about in the year you reached this milestone.

- ✦ National speed limits set at 55 mph
- ✦ Volcano in Alaska "erupts" in April Fool
- ✦ Nixon resigns
- ✦ President Ford pardons Nixon
- ✦ Miami Dolphins repeat Super Bowl victory
- ✦ 1974 Super Outbreak tornadoes hit 13 states
- ✦ Hank Aaron breaks Babe Ruth's homerun record
- ✦ Expo' '74 World Fair opens
- ✦ Impeachment proceedings proceed against the president (right)
- ✦ First barcode scanned
- ✦ Franklin National Bank collapses
- ✦ Oakland A's win third consecutive World Series
- ✦ Muhammad Ali wins the "Rumble in the Jungle"
- ✦ Department of Justice brings anti-trust case against AT&T
- ✦ Heiress Patricia Hearst kidnapped
- ✦ 10-month Daylight Savings Time to save energy amid oil embargo
- ✦ Work begins on Alaska Oil pipeline
- ✦ MRI scanner developed
- ✦ Chris Evert wins at Wimbledon
- ✦ Jimmy Connors wins at Wimbledon and US Open
- ✦ G.I. Joe doll gets his "kung fu grip"
- ✦ All NHL goalies begin wearing facemasks
- ✦ Post-it notes created
- ✦ Tourists allowed into Fort Knox

Born this year:
- ꝏ TV hosts Jimmy Fallon and Ryan Seacrest
- ꝏ Actor Leonardo DiCaprio
- ꝏ Actress Hilary Swank
- ꝏ Rapper Nelly

Mary Evans / The Everett Collection

Rose Mary Woods was the loyal personal secretary to President Nixon and took responsibility for the gap of more than 18 minutes in the White House tapes. How did it happen? Above, she recreates the incident in which she said she received a phone call and in doing so accidentally hit the erase button while simultaneously keeping her foot on the pedal of the transcription machine. She is then said to have maintained this awkward position—which came to be known as the "Rose Mary Stretch"—for the five-minute duration of the phone call. She couldn't explain the remaining gaps in the tape.

US Open Champions

Winners while you were between the ages of the youngest (John McDermott, 1911, 19 years) and the oldest (Hale Irwin,1990, at 45). Planning a win? Better hurry up!

1975	Lou Graham
1976	Jerry Pate
1977	Hubert Green
1978	Andy North
1979	Hale Irwin
1980	**Jack Nicklaus**

Nicklaus set the record for years (18) between the first and last US Open victory.

1981	David Graham
1982	Tom Watson
1983	Larry Nelson
1984	Fuzzy Zoeller
1985	Andy North
1986	Raymond Floyd
1987	Scott Simpson
1988	Curtis Strange
1989	Curtis Strange
1990	Hale Irwin
1991	Payne Stewart
1992	Tom Kite
1993	Lee Janzen
1994	Ernie Els
1995	Corey Pavin
1996	Steve Jones
1997	Ernie Els
1998	Lee Janzen
1999	Payne Stewart
2000	**Tiger Woods**

Woods won by 15 strokes, the largest margin ever.

2001	Retief Goosen

Popular Girls' Names

20

If you started a family at a young age, these are the names you're most likely to have chosen. And even if you didn't pick them, a lot of Americans did!

Jennifer

Amy

Melissa

Heather

Angela

The third year in fifth place for Angela: her highest ranking.

Michelle

Kimberly

Jessica

Lisa

Amanda

Stephanie

Rebecca

Nicole

Christina

Sarah

Elizabeth

Shannon

Jamie

1976 was a high point for girl's name Jamie, but also saw Jaime appear from out of the blue, in 29th place. (By 1980, she was gone).

Kelly

Laura

Julie

Mary

Rachel

Erin

Andrea

Rising and falling stars:

Courtney, Natalie, Samantha and Mandy made an entrance; Donna, Deborah and Barbara bid us adieu.

Animals Extinct in Your Lifetime

Billions of passenger pigeons once flew the US skies. By 1914, they had been trapped to extinction. Not every species dies at our hands, but it's a sobering roll-call. (Date is year last known alive or declared extinct).

1960	Candango mouse, Brasilia
1962	Red-bellied opossum, Argentina
1963	Kākāwahie honeycreeper, Hawaii
1964	South Island snipe, New Zealand
1966	Arabian ostrich
1967	Saint Helena earwig
1967	**Yellow blossom pearly mussel** Habitat loss and pollution proved terminal for this Tennessee resident.
1968	Mariana fruit bat (Guam)
1971	Lake Pedder earthworm, Tasmania
1972	Bushwren, New Zealand
1977	Siamese flat-barbelled catfish, Thailand
1979	Yunnan Lake newt, China
1981	Southern gastric-brooding frog, Australia
1986	Las Vegas dace
1989	Golden toad (see right)
1990	Dusky seaside sparrow, East Coast USA
1990	Atitlán grebe, Guatemala
1990s	Rotund rocksnail, USA
2000	**Pyrenean ibex, Iberia** For a few minutes in 2003 this species was brought back to life through cloning, but sadly the newborn female ibex died.
2001	Caspian tiger, Central Asia
2008	Saudi gazelle
2012	**Pinta giant tortoise** The rarest creature in the world for the latter half of his 100-year life, Lonesome George of the Galapagos was the last remaining Pinta tortoise.
2016	Bramble Cay melomys (a Great Barrier Reef rodent)

The observed history of the golden toad is brief and tragic. It wasn't discovered until 1964, abundant in a pristine area of Costa Rica. By 1989 it had gone, a victim of rising temperatures.

Popular Boys' Names

Here are the top boys' names for this year. Many of the most popular choices haven't shifted much since you were born, but more modern names are creeping in…

Michael
Jason
Christopher
David
James
John
Robert
Brian

For eight years from 1972, Brian was lodged at eighth place, his best performance. He's dependable, is Brian.

Matthew
Daniel
William
Joseph
Eric
Jeremy
Kevin
Ryan
Jeffrey
Joshua
Richard
Steven
Timothy
Anthony
Thomas
Scott
Mark
Charles
Andrew

Rising and falling stars:

While Bobby, Shannon and Marc were off, Gabriel, Jeremiah and Zachary had arrived in style.

Popular Movies When You Were 21

The biggest stars in the biggest movies: these are the films the nation were enjoying as you entered into adulthood.

Annie Hall 🎟 Woody Allen, Diane Keaton, Tony Roberts

The Other Side of Midnight 🎟 Marie-France Pisier, John Beck, Susan Sarandon

Herbie Goes to Monte Carlo 🎟 Dean Jones, Don Knotts, Julie Sommars

Heroes 🎟 Henry Winkler, Sally Field, Harrison Ford

Close Encounters of the Third Kind 🎟 Richard Dreyfuss, Melinda Dillon, Teri Garr

High Anxiety 🎟 Mel Brooks, Madeline Kahn, Cloris Leachman

Saturday Night Fever 🎟 John Travolta, Karen Lynn Gomey, Barry Miller
Donna Pescow had to relearn her own Brooklyn accent for the role.

The Deep 🎟 Robert Shaw, Jacqueline Bisset, Nick Nolte

The Kentucky Fried Movie 🎟 George Lazenby, Bill Bixby, Henry Gibson

Which Way Is Up? 🎟 Richard Pryor, Lonette McKee, Margaret Avery

The Rescuers 🎟 Larry Clemmons, Vance Gerry, Ken Anderson

For the Love of Benji 🎟 Patsy Garrett, Benjean, Art Vasil

Slap Shot 🎟 Paul Newman, Strother Martin, Michael Ontkean

Airport '77 🎟 Jack Lemmon, Lee Grant, James Stewart

A Bridge Too Far 🎟 Sean Connery, Ryan O'Neal, Michael Caine

Smokey and the Bandit 🎟 Burt Reynolds, Sally Field, Jerry Reed
The film was a feat of improvisation after the budget was slashed just before filming began.

Semi-Tough 🎟 Burt Reynolds, Jill Clayburgh, Robert Preston

Exorcist II: The Heretic 🎟 Linda Blair, Richard Burton, Louise Fletcher

Oh, God! 🎟 George Burns, John Denver, Teri Garr

Pete's Dragon 🎟 Helen Reddy, Jim Dale, Mickey Rooney

Star Wars Ep. IV: A New Hope 🎟 Mark Hamill, Harrison Ford, Carrie Fisher

MacArthur 🎟 Gregory Peck, Ed Flanders, Dan O'Herlihy

Across the Nation

A selection of national headlines from the year you turned 21. But how many can you remember?

+ VHS machines arrive on the market
+ Apple II released
+ President Jimmy Carter inaugurated (right)
+ Atari 2600 gaming system released
+ Son of Sam killer arrested
+ NASA launches Voyager I and Voyager II
+ New York City blackout
+ Elvis Presley died
+ Authority over Panama Canal returned to Panama
+ Trans Alaska Pipeline starts pumping oil
+ Beverly Hills Supper Club catches fire
+ President Carter pardons Vietnam draft dodgers
+ President Carter warns about curtailing oil consumption
+ Seattle Slew wins the Triple Crown
+ Dam in Georgia fails, killing 39 people
+ First GPS signal received and decoded
+ Space Shuttle makes first test flight
+ Commodore PET begins sales
+ Radio Shack offers TRS-80 to consumers
+ Comedian Steve Martin asks to be excused
+ I love New York ad begins
+ Two baseball players first give each other a "high five"
+ Snow falls in Miami for the first and last known time
+ A.J. Foyt takes 1st place in the Indy 500 for the 4th time
+ Disco craze takes America

Born this year:
⚭ Rapper Kanye West
⚭ Boxer Floyd Mayweather Jr.
⚭ Author John Green
⚭ Actress Liv Tyler

"Jimmy Who is Running for What!?" a newspaper in Jimmy Carter's home state of Georgia asked after he announced his intention to run for president. But an effective national strategy, his status as an "outsider" and favorable media coverage took the former peanut farmer and nuclear physicist all the way to the White House.

The Biggest Hits When You Were 21

The artists you love at 21 are with you for life. How many of these hits from this milestone year can you still hum or sing in the tub?

Leo Sayer 🎤 When I Need You

Fleetwood Mac 🎤 Dreams

Thelma Houston 🎤 Don't Leave Me This Way

The Marshall Tucker Band 🎤 Heard It in a Love Song

David Soul 🎤 Don't Give Up on Us

The Eagles 🎤 Hotel California

Glen Campbell 🎤 Southern Nights

The Bee Gees 🎤 Stayin' Alive

The Emotions 🎤 Best of My Love

Queen 🎤 We Are the Champions

Rose Royce 🎤 Car Wash

Crystal Gayle 🎤 Don't It Make
My Brown Eyes Blue

Eric Clapton 🎤 Lay Down Sally

Linda Ronstadt 🎤 Blue Bayou

Stevie Wonder 🎤 Sir Duke

Bonnie Tyler 🎤 It's a Heartache

The Floaters 🎤 Float On

Kenny Rogers 🎤 Lucille

Bill Conti 🎤 Gonna Fly Now
(Theme from Rocky)

Marvin Gaye 🎤 Got to Give It Up (Part 1)

Supertramp 🎤 Give a Little Bit

The Commodores 🎤 Brick House

Dolly Parton 🎤 Here You Come Again

Al Stewart 🎤 Year of the Cat

Popular Food in the 1960s

Changes in society didn't stop at the front door: a revolution in the kitchen brought us exotic new recipes, convenience in a can, and even space-age fruit flavors. These are the tastes of a decade, but how many of them were on the menu for your family?

McDonald's Big Mac
First served in 1967 by a Pittsburgh franchisee.
Royal Shake-a-Pudd'n Dessert Mix
Tunnel of Fudge Cake
Campbell's SpaghettiOs
Pop-Tarts
B&M's canned bread
Cool Whip
A time-saving delight that originally contained no milk or cream, meaning that it could be frozen and transported easily.

Grasshopper pie
Beech-Nut Fruit Stripe Gum
Sandwich Loaf
Lipton Onion Soup Dip
Millions of packets are still sold each year of this favorite that was once known as "Californian Dip".

Jello salad
Hires Root Beer
Baked Alaska
Tang
Invented by William A. Mitchell who also concocted Cool Whip, Tang was used by astronauts to flavor the otherwise unpalatable water on board the Gemini and Apollo missions.

Corn Diggers
Teem soda
Eggo Waffles
Kraft Shake 'N Bake
Maypo oatmeal
In 1985, Dire Straights sang, "I want my MTV"—an echo of the stars who'd shouted the same words to promote the new station. But 30 years before that (and the inspiration for MTV's campaign), an animated child yelled, "I want my Maypo!"

Fashion in the Sixties

As a child, you (generally) wear what you're given. It's only in hindsight, on fading Polaroids, that you recognize that your outfits carried the fashion imprint of the day. Whether you were old or bold enough to carry off a pair of bell bottoms, though, is a secret that should remain between you and your photo albums.

Bell bottoms
Bell bottoms were widely available at Navy surplus and thrift stores at a time when second-hand shopping was on the rise.

Miniskirts and mini dresses

Peasant blouses

Rudi Gernreich
Pope Paul IV banned Catholics from wearing his monokini—
a topless swim suit.

US flag clothing

Tulle turbans

Shift dresses

Collarless jackets
This jacket trend was popularized by the Beatles in 1963.

Babydoll dresses

V-neck tennis sweaters

Afghan coats

Leopard print clothing
In 1962, Jackie Kennedy wore a leopard print coat which caused a spike in demand for leopard skin, leading to the death of up to 250,000 leopards. The coat's designer, Oleg Cassini, felt guilty about it for the rest of his life.

Tie-dye clothing

Short, brightly colored, shapeless dresses

Pillbox hats

Mary Quant

Maxi skirts

Bonnie Cashin

Plaid

Poor boy sweaters

Pea coats

Around the World When You Turned 25

With the growing reach of news organizations, events from outside our borders were sometimes front-page news. How many do you remember?

- Prince Charles marries Lady Diana
- Soviets launch Venera 13 spacecraft
- Poland declares martial law
- Pope John Paul II shot
- London Marathon begins
- European high-speed rail service begins
- Yorkshire Ripper is arrested
- Last country bans slaves
- Anwar Sadat is assassinated
- Earthquake hits Athens
- Riots occur in several UK cities
- Marcos lifts martial law in the Philippines
- Attempted coup in Bangladesh
- Antigua gains independence
- Passenger ship sinks in Java Sea
- Pinochet declares himself president of Chile
- Mitterrand becomes president of France
- Train disaster kills hundreds in India
- Israeli jets destroy reactor in Iraq
- Beirut is bombed by Israel
- Panda born in Mexico City Zoo
- Bob Marley dies
- Belize gains independence
- Iraq embassy is bombed in Beirut
- China's population reaches 1 billion

Cars of the 1960s

Smaller cars. More powerful cars. More distinctive cars. More variety, yes: but the success of imported models such as the Volkswagen Beetle was a sign that more fundamental changes lay ahead for The Big Three.

1940	Ford Lincoln Continental
1949	Volkswagen Beetle
1950	Volkswagen Type 2 (Microbus)
1958	**General Motors Chevrolet Impala** In 1965, the Impala sold more than 1 million units, the most sold by any model in the US since WWII.
1958	American Motors Corporation Rambler Ambassador
1959	General Motors Chevrolet El Camino
1959	Ford Galaxie
1960	**Ford Falcon** The cartoon strip "Peanuts" was animated for TV to market the Falcon.
1960	General Motors Pontiac Tempest
1960	General Motors Chevrolet Corvair
1961	**Jaguar E-Type** Ranked first in The Daily Telegraph UK's list of the world's "100 most beautiful cars" of all time.
1961	Chrysler Newport
1962	Shelby Cobra
1963	General Motors Buick Riviera
1963	Porsche 911
1963	Kaiser-Jeep Jeep Wagoneer
1964	**Ford Mustang** The song of the same name reached #6 on the R&B Charts in 1966. That year, more Ford Mustangs were sold (550,000) than any other car.
1964	General Motors Chevrolet Chevelle
1964	Chrysler Plymouth Barracuda
1964	General Motors Pontiac GTO
1967	General Motors Chevrolet Camaro
1967	Ford Mercury Cougar
1968	Chrysler Plymouth Road Runner

Books of the Decade

Were you a voracious bookworm in your twenties? Or a more reluctant reader, only drawn by the biggest titles of the day? Here are the new titles that fought for your attention.

1976	Roots by Alex Haley
1976	The Hite Report by Shere Hite
1977	The Thorn Birds by Colleen McCullough
1977	The Women's Room by Marilyn French
1978	Eye of the Needle by Ken Follett
1978	The World According to Garp by John Irving
1979	Flowers in the Attic by V.C. Andrews
1979	The Hitchhiker's Guide to the Galaxy by Douglas Adams
1979	Sophie's Choice by William Styron
1980	Rage of Angels by Sidney Sheldon
1980	The Bourne Identity by Robert Ludlum
1980	The Covenant by James Michener
1981	The Hotel New Hampshire by John Irving
1981	Noble House by James Clavell
1981	An Indecent Obsession by Colleen McCullough
1982	The Color Purple by Alice Walker
1982	Space by James A. Michener
1983	Pet Sematary by Stephen King
1983	Hollywood Wives by Jackie Collins
1984	You Can Heal Your Life by Louise Hay
1984	Money: A Suicide Note by Martin Amis
1985	The Handmaid's Tale by Margaret Atwood
1985	White Noise by Don DeLillo
1985	Lake Wobegon Days by Garrison Keillor

Prominent Americans

This new set of definitive stamps, issued from 1965 onwards, aimed to do a better job of capturing the diversity of the Americans who made a nation. The series doubled the previous number of women depicted...to two. How many did you have in your collection?

Thomas Jefferson 1 ¢ Third US President
Albert Gallatin 1 ¼ ¢ Fourth Treasury Secretary
Frank Lloyd Wright 2 ¢ Architect
Francis Parkman 3 ¢ Historian
Abraham Lincoln 4 ¢ 16th US President
George Washington 5 ¢ First US President
Franklin D Roosevelt 6 ¢ 32nd US President
Dwight Eisenhower 6 / 8 ¢ 34th US President
In 1957, Eisenhower became the first president to travel by helicopter instead of a limo, en route to Camp David (which he had called Shangri-La, but renamed after his grandson).

Benjamin Franklin 7 ¢ Polymath
Albert Einstein 8 ¢ Physicist
Andrew Jackson 10 ¢ 7th US President
Henry Ford 12 ¢ Founder of Ford Motor Company
John F. Kennedy 13 ¢ 35th US President
Fiorello LaGuardia 14 ¢ Mayor of New York City in WWII
Read Dick Tracy comics on the radio during a paper strike.

Oliver Wendell Holmes, Jr 15 ¢ Supreme Court Justice
Ernie Pyle 16 ¢ Journalist during World War II
Elizabeth Blackwell 18 ¢ First woman to get a medical degree.
After 11 college rejections, male students at Geneva Medical College all voted for her acceptance. They did it as a joke.

George C Marshall 20 ¢ Sec. of State and Sec. of Defense
Amadeo Giannini 21 ¢ Founder of Bank of America
Frederick Douglass 25 ¢ Slavery escapee, abolitionist leader
John Dewey 30 ¢ Educational pioneer
Thomas Paine 40 ¢ Helped inspire the American Revolution
Lucy Stone 50 ¢ Suffragist and slavery campaigner
Eugene O'Neill $1 Playwright
John Bassett Moore $5 Jurist

Sixties Game Shows

Recovery from the quiz show scandal of the fifties was a gradual process. Big prize money was out; games were in—the sillier the better, or centered around relationships. "Popcorn for the mind," as game show creator Chuck Barris memorably put it.

College Bowl 🏆 (1953-70)
Snap Judgment 🏆 (1967-69)
To Tell The Truth 🏆 (1956-present)
Dough Re Mi 🏆 (1958-60)
Camouflage 🏆 (1961-62 & 1980)
Dream House 🏆 (1968-84)
Say When!! 🏆 (1961-65)
Let's Make A Deal 🏆 (1963-present)
The long-time presenter of the show, Monty Hall, gave rise to the eponymous problem: when one door in three hides a prize and you've made your pick, should you change your answer when the host reveals a "zonk" (dud) behind another door? (The counterintuitive answer is yes!)

Your First Impression 🏆 (1962-64)
Supermarket Sweep 🏆 (1965-present)
In one of its many comebacks, 1990 episodes of Supermarket Sweep featured monsters roaming the aisles including Frankenstein and Mr. Yuk.

You Don't Say! 🏆 1963-79)
It's Your Bet 🏆 (1969-73)
Yours For A Song 🏆 (1961-63)
Concentration 🏆 (1958-91)
Seven Keys 🏆 (1960-65)
Queen For A Day 🏆 1945-1970)
Password 🏆 (1961-75)
Video Village 🏆 (1960-62)
Who Do You Trust? 🏆 (1957-63)
Originally titled, "Do You Trust Your Wife?"
Personality 🏆 (1967-69)
Beat The Odds 🏆 (1961-69)

Across the Nation

Another decade passes and you're well into adulthood. Were you reading the news, or making it? Here are the national stories that dominated the front pages.

✦ Space Shuttle Challenger destroyed moments after launch (right)
✦ Lazer Tag games begin
✦ American Girl dolls released
✦ New York Mets win the World Series
✦ Chicago Bears become Super Bowl champions
✦ Journalist Geraldo Rivera finds Al Capone's vault empty
✦ 5 million united for Hands Across America charity event
✦ Public transport bans smoking
✦ Iran-Contra Affair begins
✦ Mike Tyson becomes Heavyweight Champion
✦ Tax reform legislation enacted
✦ IBM reveals the 12lbs laptop
✦ Human Genome Project launched
✦ Revolutionary 386 microprocessor introduced
✦ Nicotine patch released
✦ Statue of Liberty reopens after renovation
✦ Postal worker kills 14 fellow workers
✦ Rock and Roll Hall of Fame begins inducting musicians
✦ Actor Clint Eastwood elected mayor of Carmel, California
✦ Singer Tina Turner receives her star on the Walk of Fame
✦ Instant replay comes to the NFL
✦ President Reagan meets with Soviet's Gorbachev
✦ Federal government shuts down because of budget dispute
✦ Fox Broadcasting Company begins

Born this year:
👶 Singer Lady Gaga
👶 Actress Lindsay Lohan
👶 American footballer Michael Oher

NASA

Just 73 seconds after the launch of Space Shuttle Challenger on the morning of January 28th, the unimaginable happened. A cold-weather failure of an O-ring seal led to a catastrophe witnessed by millions. Seven astronauts died: Michael Smith, Dick Scobee, Judith Resnik, Ronald McNair, Ellison Onizuka, Gregory Jarvis, and school teacher Christa McAuliffe. To the many children who saw the event, President Reagan told them, "I know it is hard to understand, but sometimes painful things happen ... The Challenger crew was pulling us into the future, and we'll continue to follow them."

The Biggest Hits When You Were 30...

How many of these big tunes from the year you turned thirty will still strike a chord decades later?

Robert Palmer 🎸 Addicted to Love

Berlin 🎸 Take My Breath Away

Atlantic Starr 🎸 Secret Lovers

Madonna 🎸 Papa Don't Preach

Dionne Warwick and Friends 🎸 That's What Friends Are For

Mister Mister 🎸 Broken Wings

Crystal Gayle 🎸 Cry

Simply Red 🎸 Holding Back the Years

Eddie Money 🎸 Take Me Home Tonight

Lionel Richie 🎸 Say You, Say Me

Hank Williams Jr. 🎸 Ain't Misbehavin'

Janet Jackson 🎸 What Have You Done
for Me Lately

Peter Gabriel 🎸 Sledgehammer

Patti LaBelle
and Michael McDonald 🎸 On My Own

The Georgia Satellites 🎸 Keep Your Hands to Yourself

Steve Winwood 🎸 Higher Love

Timex Social Club 🎸 Rumors

Dan Seals 🎸 Bop

Kenny Loggins 🎸 Danger Zone

The Jets 🎸 Crush on You

Bon Jovi 🎸 You Give Love a Bad Name

Howard Jones 🎸 No One Is to Blame

Run DMC featuring Aerosmith 🎸 Walk This Way

John Cougar Mellencamp 🎸 R.O.C.K. in the USA

...and the Movies You Saw That Year, Too

From award winners to crowd pleasers, here are the movies that played as your third decade drew to a close.

Stand by Me Wil Wheaton, River Phoenix, Corey Feldman
Before choosing Richard Dreyfuss, Rob Reiner considered David Dukes, Ted Bessell, and Michael McKean for the role of narrator.

Peggy Sue Got Married Kathleen Turner, Nicolas Cage, Barry Miller
Aliens Sigourney Weaver, Carrie Henn, Michael Biehn
Ferris Bueller's Day Off Matthew Broderick, Alan Ruck, Mia Sara
The Color of Money Paul Newman, Tom Cruise
Karate Kid, Part II Ralph Macchio, Noriyuki "Pat" Morita, Nobu McCarthy
Hannah and Her Sisters Mia Farrow, Dianne Wiest, Michael Caine
Star Trek IV: The Voyage Home William Shatner, Leonard Nimoy, DeForest Kelley
Short Circuit Ally Sheedy, Steve Guttenberg, Fisher Stevens
Platoon Tom Berenger, Willem Dafoe, Charlie Sheen
Police Academy 3 Steve Guttenberg, Bubba Smith, David Graf
Top Gun Tom Cruise, Tim Robbins, Kelly McGillis
The film is dedicated to Art Scholl, the stunt pilot who died during filming.

Ruthless People Danny DeVito, Bette Midler, Judge Reinhold
Down and Out in Beverly Hills Nick Nolte, Bette Midler, Richard Dreyfuss
Pretty in Pink Molly Ringwald, Jon Cryer, Harry Dean Stanton
Crocodile Dundee Paul Hogan, Linda Kozlowski, John Meillon
Back to School Rodney Dangerfield, Keith Gordon, Sally Kellerman
Running Scared Gregory Hines, Billy Crystal, Steven Bauer
An American Tail Cathianne Blore, Dom DeLuise, Phillip Glasser
The Money Pit Tom Hanks, Shelley Long, Alexander Godunov
The Golden Child Eddie Murphy, Charlotte Lewis, Charles Dance
Nothing in Common Tom Hanks, Jackie Gleason, Eva Marie Saint

Around the House

Sometimes with a fanfare but often by stealth, inventions and innovations transformed the 20th-century household. Here's what arrived between the ages of 10 and 30.

1966	Doritos tortilla chips
1967	Close-up toothpaste
1968	Bean bag chair
1969	Nerf dart guns
1970	**Irish Spring soap**

Irish Spring soap's catchy tune and tag lines became part of the language with "Clean as a whistle" and "I like it too!" While it generated a lot of bad Irish accents, it has nothing to do with Ireland.

1971	Soft contact lenses
1972	Garanimal children clothes
1972	Science calculator
1973	BIC lighter
1974	Rubik's Cube
1975	Betamax video tape machine
1976	VHS video tape machine
1977	Coleco Telstar Arcade game system
1978	Cordless drill
1979	**Sony Walkman**

The Walkman was born when the co-founder of Sony wanted an easier way to listen to opera.

1980	Softsoap liquid soap
1981	IBM Personal Computer
1982	Ciabatta
1982	CD Player
1983	Dyson vacuum cleaner
1984	Sharp Nintendo Television
1985	Teddy Ruxpin talking teddy bear

Here's one that didn't quite make the grade: AT&T's Picturephone, demonstrated here at the 1964 New York World's Fair. A trial set up that year invited the public to rent two of the Picturephone rooms set up in New York, Chicago, and Washington ($16 for 3 minutes). The take-up over the following years was almost nil, but Picturephones went on sale in 1970 anyway with a prediction of a billion-dollar business by 1980. The devices were withdrawn from sale in 1973.

Female Olympic Gold Medalists in Your Lifetime

These are the women who have stood atop the podium the greatest number of times at the Summer Olympics, whether in individual or team events.

Jenny Thompson (8) ⚭ Swimming
Thompson is an anesthesiologist. She started her medical training in 2000—although she took time out while studying to win further gold World Championship medals.

Katie Ledecky (7) ⚭ Swimming
Allyson Felix (7) ⚭ Athletics
Amy Van Dyken (6) ⚭ Swimming
Dana Vollmer (5) ⚭ Swimming
Missy Franklin (5) ⚭ Swimming
Sue Bird (5) ⚭ Basketball
Diana Taurasi (5) ⚭ Basketball
The late Kobe Bryant dubbed Taurasi the "white mamba"; for others she is the G.O.A.T. in women's basketball.

Allison Schmitt (4) ⚭ Swimming
Dara Torres (4) ⚭ Swimming
Evelyn Ashford (4) ⚭ Athletics
Janet Evans (4) ⚭ Swimming
Lisa Leslie (4) ⚭ Basketball
Sanya Richards-Ross (4) ⚭ Athletics
Serena Williams (4) ⚭ Tennis
Simone Biles (4) ⚭ Gymnastics
Biles's phenomenal medal tally in Olympics and World Championships is greater than any other US gymnast.

Tamika Catchings (4) ⚭ Basketball
Teresa Edwards (4) ⚭ Basketball
Venus Williams (4) ⚭ Tennis

Around the World When You Turned 35

It's a big news day every day, somewhere in the world. Here are the stories that the media thought you'd want to read in the year of your 35th birthday.

- ✦ Kuwait is liberated from Iraq
- ✦ Cyclone in Bangladesh kills 200,000
- ✦ Soviet Union begins to break up
- ✦ Prime minister of India is assassinated
- ✦ Dead Sea Scrolls are unveiled
- ✦ UN declares sanctions on Libya
- ✦ Apartheid ends in South Africa
- ✦ Yugoslavia breaks up
- ✦ Balkan War begins
- ✦ Marxist rule ends in Ethiopia
- ✦ North Italy earthquake kills 2,000
- ✦ Powerful earthquake hits Pakistan and Afghanistan border
- ✦ Typhoon strikes Japan
- ✦ Gorbachev resigns
- ✦ Cholera epidemic hits South America
- ✦ Civil war begins in Somalia
- ✦ Coup occurs in Haiti
- ✦ Military coup overthrows Mali government
- ✦ Panama and Costa Rica hit by earthquake
- ✦ Nepal holds elections
- ✦ Volcano erupts in Japan
- ✦ Mount Pinatubo erupts in the Philippines
- ✦ West Germany moves capitol back to Berlin
- ✦ Warsaw Pact is officially dissolved
- ✦ Mauritania-Senegal Border War ends
- ✦ Ötzi the Iceman is found in the Alps
- ✦ China and Vietnam restore diplomatic relations
- ✦ Egyptian ferry sinks

Drinks of the Sixties

In the cocktail cabinet or behind the bar, these are the drinks your parents' generation were enjoying in the sixties. How many of their choices became yours when you became old enough to enjoy them?

Falstaff beer

Rusty Nail cocktail
Rumored to be a favorite drink of the Rat Pack.

Hull's Cream Ale

Stinger cocktail

Rheingold Extra Dry Lager

Gunther's Beer

Lone Star Beer

The Gimlet cocktail

The Grasshopper cocktail

Little King's Cream Ale
Best known for its miniature seven-ounce bottles.

Mai Thai cocktail

Genesee Cream Ale

Storz Beer
From Nebraska, Storz was "Brewed for the beer pro."

Iron City Beer
Iron City is reputed to have introduced the first twist-off bottle cap in 1963.

Golden Dream cocktail

Mint Julep cocktail
It's the official drink of the Kentucky Derby, with around 120,000 served over the weekend.

Koch's Light Lager Beer

Arrow 77 Beer

Daiquiri cocktail

Manhattan cocktail

Sterling Premium Pilsner

Carling Black Label

Hamm's Beer

Old fashioned cocktail

Seventies Game Shows

With enough water under the bridge since the 1950s scandals, producers of seventies game shows injected big money into new formats and revamped favorites, some of them screened five nights a week. How many did you cheer on from the couch?

High Rollers 🏆 (1974–88)

Gambit 🏆 (1972–81)

The New Treasure Hunt 🏆 (1973–82)
Perhaps the best-known episode of this show saw a woman faint when she won a Rolls Royce—that she later had to sell in order to pay the taxes.

The Cross-Wits 🏆 (1975–87)

Hollywood Squares 🏆 1966–2004)

The Newlywed Game 🏆 (1966–2013)
Show creator Chuck Barris also made "3's a Crowd"—the show in which men, their secretaries and their wives competed. The public wasn't happy.

Pyramid 🏆 (1973–present)
Thanks to inflation and rival prizes, the $10,000 Pyramid in 1973 didn't last long: from 1976 it was raised in increments to its current peak of $100,000.

Dealer's Choice 🏆 (1974–75)

Sports Challenge 🏆 (1971–79)

Tattletales 🏆 (1974–84)

It's Your Bet 🏆 (1969–73)

Celebrity Sweepstakes 🏆 (1974–77)

Rhyme and Reason 🏆 (1975–76)

Three On A Match 🏆 (1971–74)

The Match Game 🏆 (1962–present)

Sale of the Century 🏆 (1969–89)

The Dating Game 🏆 (1965–99)
The Dating Game—known as Blind Date in many international versions—saw many celebrity appearances before they became well-known, including the Carpenters and Arnold Schwarzenegger.

Popular Boys' Names

Just as middle age crept up unnoticed, so the most popular names also evolved. The traditional choices—possibly including yours—are fast losing their appeal to new parents.

Michael

Matthew

Matthew's second year as No. 2—his highest ever ranking.

Jacob

Christopher

Joshua

Nicholas

Tyler

Brandon

Austin

Andrew

Daniel

Joseph

David

Zachary

John

Ryan

James

William

Anthony

Justin

Jonathan

Alexander

Robert

Christian

Kyle

Kevin

Jordan

Thomas

Rising and falling stars:

Tristan and Isaiah are in; Corey, Peter and Gregory are out. Malik drops by as well, for one year only.

Popular Girls' Names

It's a similar story for girls' names. Increasing numbers are taking their infant inspiration from popular culture. The worlds of music, film and theater are all fertile hunting grounds for those in need of inspiration.

Emily
Emily hovered in and around the Top 100 for all of the 20th century, but only climbed the heights in the 1970s, becoming the first choice in 1996.

Jessica
Ashley
Sarah
Samantha
Taylor
Hannah
Alexis
Rachel
Elizabeth
Kayla
Megan
Amanda
Brittany
Madison
Lauren
Brianna
Victoria
Jennifer
Stephanie
Courtney
Nicole
Alyssa
Rebecca
Morgan
Alexandra
Amber

Rising and falling stars:
Say hello to Hailey; wave goodbye to Jamie and Angelica.

NBA Champions
Since You Were Born

These are the winners of the NBA Finals in your lifetime—
and the number of times they've taken the title.

- Philadelphia Warriors (1)
- **Boston Celtics (17)**
  1966: After the Lakers won Game 1 of the NBA Finals, the Celtics named their star Bill Russell player-coach. He was the first black coach in the NBA. The Celtics responded by winning the series.

- St. Louis Hawks (1)
- Philadelphia 76ers (2)
- New York Knicks (2)
- Milwaukee Bucks (2)
- **Los Angeles Lakers (12)**
  1980: With Kareem Abdul-Jabbar out with an injury, Lakers' 20-year-old rookie Magic Johnson started at center in the clinching Game 6 and scored 42 points and snared 15 rebounds.

- **Golden State Warriors (4)**
  2015: LeBron James and Stephen Curry, the stars of the teams that faced off in the 2015 NBA Finals, were both born in the same hospital in Akron, Ohio.

- Portland Trail Blazers (1)
- Washington Bullets (1)
- Seattle SuperSonics (1)
- Detroit Pistons (3)
- Chicago Bulls (6)
- Houston Rockets (2)
- San Antonio Spurs (5)
- Miami Heat (3)
- Dallas Mavericks (1)
- Cleveland Cavaliers (1)
- Toronto Raptors (1)

Fashion in the Seventies

The decade that taste forgot? Or a kickback against the sixties and an explosion of individuality? Skirts got shorter (and longer). Block colors and peasant chic vied with sequins and disco glamor. How many of your seventies outfits would you still wear today?

Wrap dresses
Diane von Fürstenberg said she invented the silent, no-zipper wrap dress for one-night stands. "Haven't you ever tried to creep out of the room unnoticed the following morning? I've done that many times."

Tube tops
Midi skirt
In 1970, fashion designers began to lower the hemlines on the mini skirt. This change wasn't welcomed by many consumers. Women picketed in New York City with "stop the midi" signs.

Track suit, running shoes, soccer jerseys
Cowl neck sweaters
His & hers matching outfits
Cork-soled platform shoes
Caftans, Kaftans, Kimonos and mummus
Prairie dresses
Cuban heels
Gaucho pants
Chokers and dog collars as necklaces
Birkenstocks
Tennis headbands
Turtleneck shirts
Puffer vests
Long knit vests layered over tops and pants
Military surplus rucksack bags
"Daisy Dukes" denim shorts
Daisy's revealing cut-off denim shorts in The Dukes of Hazzard caught the attention of network censors. The answer for actor Catherine Bach? Wear flesh-colored pantyhose—just in case.

Yves Saint Laurent
Shrink tops
Bill Gibb

Drinks of the Seventies

Breweries were bigger, and there were fewer of them. Beers were lighter. But what could you (or your parents) serve with your seventies fondue? How about a cocktail that's as heavy on the double-entendre as it was on the sloe gin? Or perhaps match the decade's disco theme with a splash of blue curaçao?

Amber Moon cocktail
Features an unbroken, raw egg and featured in the film Murder on the Orient Express.

Billy Beer

Rainier Beer

Point Special Lager

Tequila Sunrise cocktail

Regal Select Light Beer

Stroh's rum

Long Island Iced Tea cocktail

Merry Widow cocktail

Shell's City Pilsner Premium Beer

Brass Monkey cocktail

The Godfather cocktail

Brown Derby

Sea-Breeze cocktail

Schlitz
This Milwaukee brewery was the country's largest in the late sixties and early seventies. But production problems were followed by a disastrous ad campaign, and by 1981 the original brewery was closed.

Alabama Slammer cocktail

Golden Cadillac cocktail

Harvey Wallbanger cocktail

Red White & Blue Special Lager Beer

Lite Beer from Miller

Coors Banquet Beer
A beer that made the most of its initial limited distribution network by floating the idea of contraband Coors. The idea was so successful that Coors smuggling became central to the plot of the movie Smokey and the Bandit.

US Open Tennis

Across the Open Era and the US National Championship that preceded it, these men won between the year you turned 19 (matching the youngest ever champ, Pete Sampras) and 38 (William Larned's age with his seventh win, in 1911).

1975	**Manuel Orantes** Orantes came back from 5–0 down in the 4th set of the semifinal to win the 4th and 5th sets and upset top-seeded Jimmy Connors in the final.
1976	Jimmy Connors
1977	Guillermo Vilas
1978	**Jimmy Connors** Connors became the only player to win on all three surfaces that have been used by the US Open.
1979–81	John McEnroe
1982–83	Jimmy Connors
1984	John McEnroe
1985–87	Ivan Lendl Lendl was the world's number 1 player for 270 weeks during the eighties, though a win at Wimbledon eluded him. His low-key persona earned him the cutting Sports Illustrated headline, "The Champion That Nobody Cares About".
1988	Mats Wilander
1989	Boris Becker
1990	**Pete Sampras** 19-year-old Sampras became the youngest male player ever to win.
1991–92	**Stefan Edberg** Jimmy Connors made an improbable run to the 1991 US Open Semifinal at age 39. In the 1992 semifinal, Stefan Edberg and Michael Chang played the longest match ever: 5 hours, 26 minutes.
1993	Pete Sampras
1994	Andre Agassi

Books of the Decade

Family, friends, TV, and more: there are as many midlife distractions as there are books on the shelf. Did you get drawn in by these bestsellers, all published in your thirties?

1986	It by Stephen King
1986	Wanderlust by Danielle Steele
1987	Patriot Games by Tom Clancy
1987	Beloved by Toni Morrison
1987	The Bonfire of the Vanities by Tom Wolfe
1988	The Cardinal of the Kremlin by Tom Clancy
1988	The Sands of Time by Sidney Sheldon
1989	Clear and Present Danger by Stephen R. Covey
1989	The Pillars of the Earth by Ken Follett
1990	The Plains of Passage by Jean M. Auel
1990	Possession by A.S. Byatt
1990	Four Past Midnight by Stephen King
1991	The Firm by John Grisham
1991	The Kitchen God's Wife by Amy Tan
1991	Scarlett by Alexandra Ripley
1992	The Bridges of Madison County by Robert James Waller
1992	The Secret History by Donna Tartt
1993	The Celestine Prophecy by James Redfield
1993	Like Water for Chocolate by Laura Esquivel
1994	The Chamber by John Grisham
1994	Disclosure by Michael Crichton
1995	The Horse Whisperer by Nicholas Evans
1995	The Lost World by Michael Crichton
1995	The Rainmaker by John Grisham

Supreme Court Justices

These are the Supreme Court Justices appointed during your lifetime.

1956–90	William J. Brennan Jr.
1958–81	**Potter Stewart**
	Stewart is known for using the phrase "I know it when I see it" in his concurring opinion concerning potentially pornagraphic material in the Jacobellis vs. Ohio case of 1964.
1962–93	Byron White
1967–91	Thurgood Marshall
1969–86	Warren E. Burger
1970–94	Harry Blackmun
1972–87	Lewis F. Powell Jr.
1972–87	William Rehnquist
1975–2010	John Paul Stevens
1981–2006	Sandra Day O'Connor
1986–2005	**Antonin Scalia**
	Known for his strongly worded, but often funny opinions, Scalia had nine children.
1988–2018	Anthony Kennedy
1990–2009	David Souter
1991–	Clarence Thomas
1993–2020	Ruth Bader Ginsburg
1994–	Stephen Breyer
2005–	John Roberts
2006–	Samuel Alito
2009–	**Sonia Sotomayor**
	This justice is the first Hispanic member of the Supreme Court. She is a loyal New York Yankees baseball fan.
2010–	Elena Kagan
2017–	Neil Gorsuch
2018–	Brett Kavanaugh
2020–	Amy Coney Barrett

The Biggest Hits When You Were 40

Big tunes for a big birthday: how many of them enticed your middle-aged party guests onto the dance floor?

The Smashing Pumpkins 🎤 1979
Los del Rio 🎤 Macarena
Celine Dion 🎤 Because You Loved Me
Metallica 🎤 Until It Sleeps
Tracy Chapman 🎤 Give Me One Reason
The Fugees 🎤 Killing Me Softly with His Song
The Spice Girls 🎤 Wannabe
LeAnn Rimes 🎤 Blue
Toni Braxton 🎤 You're Makin' Me High
Collective Soul 🎤 The World I Know
Eric Clapton 🎤 Change the World
Patty Loveless 🎤 You Can Feel Bad
Oasis 🎤 Champagne Supernova
No Doubt 🎤 Don't Speak
Blues Traveler 🎤 Hook
Mindy McCready 🎤 Guys Do It All the Time
Blackstreet featuring Dr. Dre 🎤 No Diggity
Primitive Radio Gods 🎤 Standing Outside a Broken Phone Booth with Money in My Hand
Brooks and Dunn 🎤 My Maria
R. Kelly 🎤 I Believe I Can Fly
Dave Matthews Band 🎤 Crash Into Me
Jewel 🎤 Who Will Save Your Soul
George Strait 🎤 Blue Clear Sky
BoDeans 🎤 Closer to Free

Popular Food in the 1970s

From fads to ads, here's a new collection of dinner party dishes and family favorites. This time it's the seventies that's serving up the delights—and some of us are still enjoying them today!

Watergate Salad
Black Forest cake
Chex Mix
Cheese Tid-Bits
Dolly Madison Koo-koos (cupcakes)

Life Cereal
"I'm not gonna try it. You try it. Let's get Mikey…he hates everything." Three on- and off-screen brothers, one memorable ad that ran for much of the seventies.

The Manwich
"A sandwich is a sandwich, but a manwich is a meal," the ads announced in 1969.

Tomato aspic
Bacardi rum cake
Impossible pies
Zucchini bread
Oscar Mayer bologna
Poke Cake made with Jell-O
Libbyland Dinners

Reggie! Bar
Named after New York Yankees' right fielder Reggie Jackson and launched as a novely, Reggie! Bars were on sale for six years.

Hostess Chocodiles
Polynesian chicken salad
Salmon mousse
Cheese log appetizer
Gray Poupon Dijon Mustard

Tootsie Pop
So how many licks does it take to get to the center of a Tootsie Pop? 364, and that's official: it was tested on a "licking machine."

Cars of the 1970s

A decade of strikes, federal regulations, foreign imports, oil crises, safety and quality concerns: car sales were up overall, but the US industry was under pressure like never before. Iconic new models to debut include the Pontiac Firebird and the outrageous, gold-plated Stutz Blackhawk.

1940	**Chrysler New Yorker** When is a New Yorker not a New Yorker? The eighth generation of this upscale car bore little resemblance to the 1940 launch models. Yet in 1970, the New Yorker was barely middle-aged: they lived on until 1997.
1948	Ford F-Series
1959	General Motors Cadillac Coupe de Ville
1959	Chrysler Plymouth Valiant
1960	Chrysler Dodge Dart
1961	**General Motors Oldsmobile Cutlass** The Cutlass outsold any other model in US for four consecutive years, notching up nearly 2 million sales.
1962	General Motors Chevrolet Nova
1965	General Motors Chevrolet Caprice
1965	Ford LTD
1967	General Motors Pontiac Firebird
1968	BMW 2002
1970	Chrysler Dodge Challenger
1970	General Motors Chevrolet Monte Carlo
1970	General Motors Chevrolet Vega
1970	American Motors Corporation Hornet
1970	Ford Maverick
1971	Nissan Datsun 240Z
1971	**Stutz Blackhawk** These luxury automobiles started at a cool $22,000 ($150,000 today); the first car sold went to Elvis. Among the many other celebrity Blackhawk owners was Dean Martin; one of his three models sported the vanity plate DRUNKY. He crashed it.
1971	Ford Pinto
1973	Honda Civic
1975	Ford Granada
1978	Ford Fiesta

US Banknotes

The cast of US banknotes hasn't changed in your lifetime, giving you plenty of time to get to know them. (Although if you have a lot of pictures of James Madison and Salmon P. Chase around the house, you might want to think about a visit to the bank.)

Fifty cent paper coin (1862-1876) Abraham Lincoln
These bills were known as "shinplasters" because the quality of the paper was so poor that they could be used to bandage leg wounds during the Civil War.

One dollar bill (1862-1869) Salmon P. Chase
The US Secretary of Treasury during Civil War, Salmon P. Chase is credited with putting the phrase "In God we trust" on US currency beginning in 1864.

One dollar bill (1869-present) George Washington
Some bills have a star at the end of the serial number. This means they are replacement bills for those printed with errors.

One silver dollar certificate (1886-96) Martha Washington
Two dollar bill (1862-present) Thomas Jefferson
Two dollar bills have a reputation of being rare, but there are actually 600 million in circulation in the US.

Five dollar bill (1914-present) Abraham Lincoln
Ten dollar bill (1914-1929) Andrew Jackson
Ten dollar bill (1929-present) Alexander Hamilton
Twenty dollar bill (1865-1869) Pocahontas
Twenty dollar bill (1914-1929) Grover Cleveland
Twenty dollar bill (1929-present) Andrew Jackson
Fifty dollar bill (1914-present) Ulysses S. Grant
One hundred dollar bill (1914-1929) Benjamin Franklin
The one hundred dollar bill has an expected circulation life of 22.9 years while the one dollar bill has an expected circulation life of just 6.6 years.

Five hundred dollar bill (1918-1928) John Marshall
Five hundred dollar bill (1945-1969) William McKinley
One thousand dollar bill (1918-1928) Alexander Hamilton
One thousand dollar bill (1928-1934) Grover Cleveland
Five thousand dollar bill (1918-1934) James Madison
Ten thousand dollar bill (1928-1934) Salmon P. Chase

Male Olympic Gold Medalists in Your Lifetime

These are the male athletes that have scooped the greatest number of individual and team gold medals at the Summer Olympics in your lifetime.

Michael Phelps (23) 🏊 Swimming (right)

Carl Lewis (9) 🏊 Athletics

Mark Spitz (9) 🏊 Swimming

For 36 years, Spitz's 7-gold-medal haul at the 1972 Munich Olympics was unbeaten; Michael Phelps finally broke the spell with his eighth gold in Beijing.

Matt Biondi (8) 🏊 Swimming

Caeleb Dressel (7) 🏊 Swimming

Ryan Lochte (6) 🏊 Swimming

Don Schollander (5) 🏊 Swimming

Gary Hall Jr. (5) 🏊 Swimming

Aaron Peirsol (5) 🏊 Swimming

Nathan Adrian (5) 🏊 Swimming

Tom Jager (5) 🏊 Swimming

Al Oerter Jr. (4) 🏊 Athletics

Four out of four: Oerter won Olympic gold medals in the discus in every Games from 1956–1968. He fought injuries that required him to wear a neck brace for the 1964 Tokyo Olympics—but he still set an Olympic record.

Greg Louganis (4) 🏊 Diving

Jason Lezak (4) 🏊 Swimming

John Naber (4) 🏊 Swimming

Jon Olsen (4) 🏊 Swimming

Lenny Krayzelburg (4) 🏊 Swimming

Matt Grevers (4) 🏊 Swimming

Michael Johnson (4) 🏊 Athletics

Once the fastest man in the world over 200 meters, Johnson took 15 minutes to walk the same distance in 2018 following a mini-stroke—but took it as a sign that he'd make a full recovery.

Between 2000 and 2016, Michael Phelps won 28 Olympic medals, including 23 gold and 16 for individual events. That's 10 more than his nearest competitor, Larisa Latynina, a gymnast of the Soviet Union who took her last gold medal fifty years earlier.

Winter Olympics Venues Since You Were Born

Unless you're an athlete or winter sports fan, the Winter Olympics can slip past almost unnoticed. These are the venues; can you remember the host countries and years? (Answers at the bottom of the page!)

Lillehammer
Cortina d'Ampezzo
Salt Lake City
Sapporo
Albertville
Turin
Grenoble
Sarajevo
Lake Placid
Sochi
Innsbruck
Squaw Valley
Nagano
Calgary
Innsbruck
Vancouver
PyeongChang

Answers: Lillehammer: Norway, 1994; Cortina d'Ampezzo: Italy, 1956; Salt Lake City: USA, 2002; Sapporo: Japan, 1972; Albertville: France, 1992; Turin: Italy, 2006; Grenoble: France, 1968; Sarajevo: Yugoslavia, 1984; Lake Placid: USA, 1980; Sochi: Russia, 2014; Innsbruck: Austria, 1964; Squaw Valley: USA, 1960; Nagano: Japan, 1998; Calgary: Canada, 1988; Innsbruck: Austria, 1976; Vancouver: Canada, 2010; PyeongChang: South Korea, 2018

Fashion in the Eighties

Eighties fashion was many things, but subtle wasn't one of them. Influences were everywhere from aerobics to Wall Street, from pop princesses to preppy polo shirts. The result was chaotic, but fun. How many eighties throwbacks still lurk in your closet?

Stirrup pants
Ralph Lauren
Ruffled shirts
Jean Paul Gaultier
Acid wash jeans
Stone washing had been around a while, but the acid wash trend came about by chance—Rifle jeans of Italy accidentally tumbled jeans, bleach, and pumice stone with a little water. The result? A fashion craze was born.

Camp collar shirt with horizontal stripes
Thierry Mugler
Oversized denim jackets
Scrunchies
"Members Only" jackets
Members Only military-inspired jackets were marketed with the tagline "When you put it on...something happens."

Paper bag waist pants
Pleated stonewash baggy jeans
Cut-off sweatshirts/hoodies
Vivienne Westwood
Azzedine Alaia
Shoulder pads
Dookie chains
Leg warmers
Bally shoes
Jordache jeans
Calvin Klein
Windbreaker jackets
Ray-Ban Wayfarer sunglasses
Popularized by Tom Cruise in the movie Risky Business.

Parachute pants
Jumpsuits

World Buildings

Some of the most striking and significant buildings in the world sprang up when you were between 25 and 50 years old. How many do you know?

1981	Sydney Tower
1982	First Canadian Centre, Calgary
1983	Teresa Carreño Cultural Complex, Caracus
1984	Deutsche Bank Twin Towers, Frankfurt
1985	Exchange Square, Hong Kong
1986	**Baha'i Lotus Temple, New Delhi** The Lotus Temple is open to all faiths to come worship, but no images, pictures, sermons, or even musical instruments are permitted.
1987	Fuji Xerox Towers, Singapore
1988	Canterra Tower, Calgary
1989	The Louvre Pyramid, Paris
1990	Bank of China Tower, Hong Kong
1991	One Canada Square, London
1992	Central Plaza, Hong Kong
1993	Westendstrasse 1, Frankfurt
1994	Shinjuku Park Tower, Tokyo
1995	Republic Plaza, Singapore
1996	**Petronas Twin Towers, Kuala Lampur** As iconic in Malaysia as the Eiffel Tower is in France. Its skybridge is actually two stories and is the highest of its kind in the world.
1997	Guggenheim Museum Bilbao
1998	City of Arts and Sciences, Valencia
1999	Burj Al Arab, Dubai
2000	Emirates Tower One, Dubai
2004	30 St Mary Axe (The Gherkin), London

Kentucky Derby Winners

These are the equine and human heroes from the "most exciting two minutes of sport" during your thirties and forties. Did any of them make you rich?

1986	**Ferdinand (Bill Shoemaker)** 54-year-old Bill Shoemaker became the oldest jockey to ever win the Kentucky Derby.
1987	Alysheba (Chris McCarron)
1988	Winning Colors (Gary Stevens)
1989	Sunday Silence (Pat Valenzuela)
1990	Unbridled (Craig Perret)
1991	Strike the Gold (Chris Antley)
1992	Lil E. Tee (Pat Day)
1993	Sea Hero (Jerry Bailey)
1994	Go for Gin (Chris McCarron)
1995	Thunder Gulch (Gary Stevens)
1996	Grindstone (Jerry Bailey)
1997	Silver Charm (Gary Stevens)
1998	**Real Quiet (Kent Desormeaux)** Real Quiet missed out on a Triple Crown by fractions of a second.
1999	Charismatic (Chris Antley)
2000	Fusaichi Pegasus (Kent Desormeaux)
2001	Monarchos (Jorge F. Chavez)
2002	War Emblem (Victor Espinoza)
2003	Funny Cide (Jose A. Santos)
2004	**Smarty Jones (Stewart Elliott)** Smarty Jones narrowly avoided losing his eyesight in a 2003 accident; alongside him in the 2004 Derby was the one-eyed horse Pollard's Vision, and Imperialism, a horse with poor vision in his right eye.
2005	Giacomo (Mike E. Smith)
2006	Barbaro (Edgar Prado)

World Series Champions Since You Were Born

These are the winners of the Commissioner's Trophy and the number of times they've been victorious in your lifetime.

- Detroit Tigers (2)
- New York Yankees (11)
- Cincinnati Reds (3)
- St. Louis Cardinals (5)
- Milwaukee Braves (1)
- **Los Angeles Dodgers (6)**
  1988: Dodgers' Kirk Gibson, battling injuries, hit a game-winning home run in his only at-bat of the 1988 World Series.
- Pittsburgh Pirates (3)
- Baltimore Orioles (3)
- **New York Mets (2)**
  1969: The Mets had never finished above 9th in their division.
- Oakland Athletics (4)
- Philadelphia Phillies (2)
- Kansas City Royals (2)
- **Minnesota Twins (2)**
  1991: Both teams had finished in last place the previous season.
- Toronto Blue Jays (2)
- Atlanta Braves (1)
- Florida Marlins (2)
- Arizona Diamondbacks (1)
- Anaheim Angels (1)
- Boston Red Sox (4)
- Chicago White Sox (1)
- San Francisco Giants (3)
- **Chicago Cubs (1)**
  2016: The Cubs' first World Series win since 1908.
- Houston Astros (1)
- Washington Nationals (1)

Books of the Decade

By our forties, most of us have decided what we like to read. But occasionally a book can break the spell, revealing the delights of other genres. Did any of these newly published books do that for you?

1996	Angela's Ashes by Frank McCourt
1996	Bridget Jones's Diary by Helen Fielding
1996	Infinite Jest by David Foster Wallace
1997	American Pastoral by Philip Roth
1997	Tuesdays with Morrie by Mitch Albom
1998	The Poisonwood Bible by Barbara Kingsolver
1998	A Man in Full by Tom Wolfe
1999	The Testament by John Grisham
1999	Hannibal by Thomas Harris
1999	Girl with a Pearl Earring by Tracy Chevalier
2000	Angels & Demons by Dan Brown
2000	Interpreter of Maladies by Jhumpa Lahiri
2000	White Teeth by Zadie Smith
2001	Life of Pi by Yann Martel
2001	The Corrections by Jonathan Franzen
2002	Everything is Illuminated by Jonathan Safran Foer
2002	The Lovely Bones by Alice Sebold
2003	The Da Vinci Code by Dan Brown
2003	The Kite Runner by Khaled Hosseini
2004	The Five People You Meet in Heaven by Mitch Albom
2004	Cloud Atlas by David Mitchell
2005	Never Let Me Go by Kazuo Ishiguro
2005	The Book Thief by Markus Zusak
2005	Twilight by Stephanie Meyer

Vice Presidents in Your Lifetime

The linchpin of a successful presidency, the best springboard to become POTUS, or both? Here are the men—and woman—who have shadowed the most powerful person in the world in your lifetime.

1953–61	Richard Nixon
1961–63	Lyndon B. Johnson
1965–69	**Hubert Humphrey**

1965–69 Hubert Humphrey

Christmas 1977: with just weeks to live, the former VP to President Johnson made goodbye calls. One was to Richard Nixon, the man who had beaten Humphrey to become president in 1968. Sensing Nixon's unhappiness at his status as Washington outcast, Humphrey invited him to take a place of honor at a funeral he knew was fast approaching.

1969–73	**Spiro Agnew (right)**
1973–74	Gerald Ford
1974–77	Nelson Rockefeller
1977–81	Walter Mondale
1981–89	**George H. W. Bush**

1981–89 George H. W. Bush

He is only the second vice president to win the presidency while holding the office of vice president.

1989-93 Dan Quayle

Quayle famously misspelled potato ("potatoe")

1993-2001 Al Gore

This VP won the Nobel Peace Prize in 2007, following in the footsteps of two other former vice presidents.

2001–09	Dick Cheney
2009–17	Joe Biden
2017–20	**Mike Pence**

2017–20 Mike Pence

In the 90s, Pence took a break from politics to become a conservative radio talk show and television host.

2020–	Kamala Harris

Spiro Agnew resigned in 1973, the second VP to quit in America's history (the first was John Calhoun in 1932). He stepped down after being charged with tax evasion and taking bribes. He covered his legal debts with a loan from friend Frank Sinatra. In 1983 he was compelled to repay $268,000: the money he had taken in bribes, plus interest.

British Prime Ministers in Your Lifetime

These are the occupants of 10 Downing Street, London, during your lifetime (not including Larry the resident cat). Don't be deceived by that unassuming black (blast-proof) door: Number 10 was originally three houses and features a warren of more than 100 rooms.

1955–57	Sir Anthony Eden
1957–63	**Harold Macmillan**

Macmillan was the scion of a wealthy publishing family. He resigned following a scandal in which a minister was found to have lied about his relationship with a 19-year-old model. Macmillan died aged 92; his last words were, "I think I will go to sleep now."

1963–64	Sir Alec Douglas-Home
1964–70	Harold Wilson
1970–74	Edward Heath
1974–76	Harold Wilson
1976–79	James Callaghan
1979–90	**Margaret Thatcher**

In 1994, Thatcher was working late in a Brighton hotel, preparing a conference speech. A bomb—planted weeks earlier by the IRA five stories above—detonated, devastating the hotel. Five were killed; Thatcher was unscathed. The conference went ahead.

1990–97	John Major
1997–2007	Tony Blair
2007–10	**Gordon Brown**

Brown has no sight in his left eye after being kicked in a school rugby game; in 2009, while Prime Minister, rips in the right retina were also diagnosed.

2010–16	David Cameron
2016–19	Theresa May
2019–	Boris Johnson

Things People Do Now (Part 2)

Imagine your ten-year-old self being given this list of today's mundane tasks and habits—and the puzzled look on your face!

+ Listen to a podcast
+ Go "viral" or become social media famous
+ Watch YouTube
+ Track the exact location of family members via your smartphone
+ Watch college football playoffs
+ Have drive-thru fast food delivered to your door
+ Check reviews before trying a new restaurant or product
+ Use LED light bulbs to save on your electric bill
+ Wear leggings as pants for any occasion
+ Use hashtags (#) to express an idea or show support
+ Join a CrossFit gym
+ Use a Forever stamp to send a letter
+ Carry a reusable water bottle
+ Work for a company with an "unlimited" paid time off policy
+ "Binge" a TV show
+ Marry a person of the same sex
+ Take your shoes off when going through airport security
+ Take a selfie
+ Use tooth-whitening strips
+ Feed babies and kids from food pouches
+ Buy recreational marijuana from a dispensary (in some states)
+ Store documents "in the cloud" and work on them from any device
+ Clean up after your pets using compostable waste bags
+ Buy free-range eggs and meat at the grocery store

A Lifetime of Technology

It's easy to lose sight of the breadth and volume of life-enhancing technology that became commonplace during the 20th Century. Here are some of the most notable advances to be made in the years you've been an adult.

1979	Compact disc
1982	**Emoticons** The inventor of the smiley emoticon hands out "Smiley" cookies every September 19th—the anniversary of the first time it was used.
1983	Internet
1986	Mir Space Station
1988	**Internet virus** The first Internet worm was specifically designed to crack passwords. Its inventor was the son of the man who invented computer passwords.
1989	World Wide Web
1992	Digital hand-sized mobile phone
1995	**Mouse with scroll wheel** Mouse scroll wheels were developed primarily as a zoom function for large Excel sheets, but became more useable as a means of scrolling.
1996	DVD player
1997	WebTV
1998	Google
1999	Wi-Fi
2000	Camera phone
2001	Wikipedia
2004	Facebook
2005	**Google Maps** Google used solar-powered cameras attached to sheep to map the Faroe Islands for Street View, or Sheep View as it became known.
2007	Apple iPhone
2007	Amazon Kindle
2009	Bitcoin
2013	Large Hadron Collider
2014	Amazon Alexa

Toys of the Sixties

The sight, feel and even smell of childhood toys leaves an indelible mark long after they've left our lives. Who can forget that metallic tang of a new Tonka toy, or the *shh-shh* noise as someone erased your masterpiece with a shake of your Etch-a-Sketch?

Chatty Cathy

G.I. Joe

Barbie's Dream House

Ken

Barbie's boyfriend made an entrance two years after we first met the billion-selling blonde doll. Ken's undewear was welded on in 1971, around the same time he acquired stick-on sideburns. What a guy.

Easy-Bake Oven

SuperBall

Lite-Brite

Hot Wheels

Rock-a-Stack

Chatter Telephone

Etch A Sketch

Thingmaker

Tonka Trucks

Johnny Seven O.M.A.

One weapon to top them all: 1964's big seller boasted functions that included an anti-tank rocket, grenade launcher and a Tommy gun.

See 'n Say

Barbie

Spirograph

Frisbee

Fred Morrison didn't invent Frisbees: that honor goes to the first person to discover that a lid is great fun to throw. But Morrison spotted the universal appeal—and the potential to make an affordable plastic version.

Slip 'n Slide

Rock 'Em Sock 'Em Robots

Grand Constructions

Governments around the world spent much of the 20th century nation building (and rebuilding), with huge civil engineering projects employing new construction techniques. Here are some of the biggest built between the ages of 25 and 50.

1981	Tjörn Bridge, Scandanavia
1982	Abu Dhabi International Airport, Abu Dhabi
1983	Queen Alia International Airport, Jordan
1984	Tennessee-Tombigbee Waterway, US
1985	Penang Bridge, Malaysia
1986	National Waterway 1, India
1987	Pikeville Cut-Through, US
1988	Great Seto Bridge, Japan
1989	Skybridge (TransLink), Canada
1990	Ningbo Lishe International Airport, China
1991	Fannefjord Tunnel, Norway
1992	Vidyasagar Setu Bridge, India
1993	Rainbow Bridge, Japan
1994	**English Channel tunnel, UK & France** Even at its predicted cost of $7 billion, the longest underwater tunnel in the world was already the most expensive project ever. By the time it opened, the bill was more than $13 billion.
1995	Denver International Airport, US
1996	Tenerife International Centre for Trade Fairs and Congresses, Spain
1997	British Library, UK
1998	SuperTerminal 1, Hong Kong
1999	**Northstar Island, US** Northstar is a five-acre artificial island created off Prudhoe Bay, Alaska. Pack ice means a conventional floating platform can't be used; during construction, an ice road brought in supplies.
2000	Hangzhou Xiaoshan International Airport, China
2004	**Millau Viaduct, France** The world's tallest bridge at 336m, the viaduct carries road traffic 270m above the valley floor.

Popular Food in the 1980s

The showy eighties brought us food to dazzle and delight. Food to make us feel good, food to share and food to go. Some innovations fell by the wayside, but many more can still be found in our baskets forty years later.

Hot Pockets

Hot Pockets were the brainchild of two brothers, originally from Iran. Their invention was launched as the Tastywich before being tweaked to become the Hot Pockets enjoyed by millions.

Bagel Bites

Crystal Light

Steak-Umms

Sizzlean Bacon

Potato skins appetizers

Tofutti ice cream

Hi-C Ecto Cooler

Hi-C has been around for a very long time, but the Ecto Cooler dates back to the Ghostbusters movie hype of the 1980s.

Hot buttered O's

Knorr Spinach Dip

Original New York Seltzer

Blondies

Blackened Redfish

The trend for blackening redfish prompted fish stocks to drop so low that commercial fishing for the species was banned in Louisiana.

Bartles & Jaymes Wine Coolers

Fruit Wrinkles

Stuffed mushrooms appetizers

TCBY Frozen Yogurt

TCBY originally stood for "This Can't Be Yogurt."

Sushi

Fajitas

Capri Sun

Jell-O Pudding Pops

Lean Cuisine frozen meals

Lean Cuisine is an FDA-regulated term, so all Lean Cuisine frozen meals need to be within the limit for saturated fat and cholesterol.

Eighties Symbols of Success

In the flamboyant era of Dallas and Dynasty there were many ways to show that you, too, had really made it. Forty years on, it's fascinating to see how some of these throwbacks are outdated or available to nearly everyone, while others are still reserved for today's wealthy peacocks.

BMW car

Cellular car phone

Rolex watch

Cosmetic surgery

In 1981 there were 1,000 liposuction procedures performed. That number increased to 250,000 by 1989.

VCR

"Home theater" projection TV

In-ground pool

AKC-registered dog

McMansion

Pagers/"beeper"

Aprica stroller

Home intercom system

Heart-shaped Jacuzzi tub

NordicTrack

This machine was originally called the Nordic Jock but was renamed due to compaints from women's rights groups.

Cruise vacation

Restaurant-standard kitchen appliances

A popular commercial stove produced enough heat to warm an average three-bedroom home. It was the energy equivalent of six residential stoves.

Ronald Reagan-style crystal jelly bean jar on your desk

Apple or Commodore 64 home computer

Volvo Station Wagon

Gordon Gekko-style "power suit"

Owning a horse or riding lessons for your children

Private jet

Tennis bracelet

Monogrammed clothes and accessories

Launched in 1980, the Apple III personal computer seen here went on sale for a hefty $4,000 and up, the equivalent of over $13,000 today. It didn't sell well and was soon withdrawn (unlike the Apple II, which went on to sell more than 5 million units).

The Transportation Coils

This novel issue of more than 50 definitive stamps first appeared on post in the early eighties, and became a favorite of collectors for its mono color engraved images of transportation methods past and present. Stamps carrying the printing plate number are particularly treasured. Here's a selection you may remember.

1 c 🖼 Omnibus
2 c 🖼 Locomotive
3 c 🖼 Handcar
4 c 🖼 **Stagecoach**

Coaches have been ferrying people and mail between US towns and cities since the late 18th century.

5 c 🖼 Motorcycle
5.5c 🖼 **Star Route Truck**

Star routes were 19th century mail routes on which carriers bid to make deliveries.

6 c 🖼 Tricycle
7.4 c 🖼 Baby Buggy
10 c 🖼 Canal Boat
11 c 🖼 Caboose
12.5 c 🖼 Pushcart
13 c 🖼 Patrol Wagon
15 c 🖼 Tugboat
17 c 🖼 Electric Auto
17 c 🖼 Dog Sled
17.5 c 🖼 Racing car
18 c 🖼 Surrey
20 c 🖼 Cog Railway
21 c 🖼 Railway Mail Car
23 c 🖼 Lunch Wagon
24.1 c 🖼 Tandem Bike
25 c 🖼 Bread Wagon
32 c 🖼 Ferry Boat
$1 🖼 **Sea Plane**

The US Navy bought its first sea plane in 1911: a Curtiss Model E, with a range of 150 miles.

Eighties Game Shows

By the eighties, game shows had their work cut out to compete against the popularity of new drama and talk shows. Still, an injection of celebrity glamour and dollar bills—alongside hours to be filled on new cable TV channels—ensured their survival. Here are the biggies.

Double Dare 🏆 (1986–2019)
Remote Control 🏆 (1987–90)
Scrabble 🏆 (1984–93)
The Price Is Right 🏆 (1972–present)
"Come on down!"—perhaps the best-known game show catchphrase of all time. One 2008 contestant was even happier than usual to do just that after 3 chips dropped into the Plinko all hit the $10,000 jackpot. Fluke? No, wires used to rig the result when filming ads hadn't been removed. She was allowed to keep the $30,000.

Family Feud 🏆 (1976–present)
Press Your Luck 🏆 (1983–86)
A show perhaps best remembered for the contestant Michael Larson, who memorized the game board and engineered a winning streak worth over $110,000. It wasn't cheating—Larson kept the winnings—but the game was swiftly reformulated.

Chain Reaction 🏆 1980–present)
Blockbusters 🏆 (1980–87)
Win, Lose, or Draw 🏆 (1987–90)
On The Spot 🏆 (1984–88)
Jeopardy! 🏆 (1964–present)
Card Sharks 🏆 (1978–present)
Wheel of Fortune 🏆 (1975–present)
Hostess Vanna White is estimated to clap 600 times a show; that's around 4,000,000 times since she began in 1982.

Fandango 🏆 (1983–88)
Body Language 🏆 (1984–86)
Jackpot! 🏆 (1974–90)

Popular Boys' Names

Not many of these boys' names were popular when you were born. But how many more of them are now in your twenty-first century family?

Noah
Fewer than ten names have ranked at No.1 since 1900, and Noah's four-year reign is among the shortest: only David has greater flash-in-the-pan status with a single year at the top back in 1960.

Liam
William
Mason
James
Benjamin
Jacob
Michael
Elijah
Ethan
Alexander
Oliver
Daniel
Lucas
Matthew
Aiden
Jackson
Logan
David
Joseph
Samuel
Henry
Owen
Sebastian
Gabriel

Rising stars:
Leonardo, Greyson and Roman are all new to the Top 100 this year.

Popular Girls' Names

60

It's a similar story for girls' names: only Elizabeth featured in the 30 most popular names for your year of birth. How long will it be before we turn full circle and Shirley, Patricia and Barbara make a comeback?

Emma
Emma has held the top slot for six years since 1900. Nobody comes close to Mary (54 years). Others: Linda (6), Lisa (8), Jennifer (15), Jessica (9), Ashley (2), Emily (12), Isabella (2), Sophia (3) and Olivia (since 2019).

Olivia
Ava
Sophia
Isabella
Mia
Charlotte
Abigail
Emily
Harper
Amelia
Evelyn
Elizabeth
Sofia
Madison
Avery
Ella
Scarlett
Grace
Chloe
Victoria
Riley
Aria
Lily
Aubrey

Rising stars:
New names we saw this year: Adeline, Luna, Kinsley, Eliana, Elena and Willow.

Game Show Hosts of the Seventies and Eighties

Here is the new generation of hosts: bow-tied, wide-smiled men to steer family favorites through tumultuous times. Astonishingly, one or two are still holding the cards.

John Charles Daly ➤◄ What's My Line (1950–1967)

Garry Moore ➤◄ To Tell The Truth (1969–1976)

Chuck Woolery ➤◄ Love Connection (1983–1994)

Bob Barker ➤◄ The Price Is Right (1972–2007)

Pat Sajak ➤◄ Wheel of Fortune (1981-)

Sajak took the crown for the longest-reigning game-show host of all time in 1983, when his 35-year reign surpassed that of Bob Barker as host of The Price is Right.

Peter Tomarken ➤◄ Press Your Luck (1983–86)

Gene Rayburn ➤◄ The Match Game (1962–1981)

Alex Trebek ➤◄ Jeopardy! (1984–2020)

At the time of his death in 2020, Trebek had hosted more than 8,200 episodes of the show.

Dick Clark ➤◄ Pyramid (1973–1988)

Richard Dawson ➤◄ Family Feud (1976–1995)

Peter Marshall ➤◄ Hollywood Squares (1966–1981)

Howard Cosell ➤◄ Battle of the Network Stars (1976–1988)

Marc Summers ➤◄ Double Dare (1986–1993)

Tom Kennedy ➤◄ Name That Tune (1974–1981)

Bert Convy ➤◄ Tattletales (1974–78; 1982–84)

Ken Ober ➤◄ Remote Control (1987–1990)

Jim Lange ➤◄ The Dating Game (1965–1980)

Wink Martindale ➤◄ Tic-Tac-Dough (1978–1985)

Art Fleming ➤◄ Jeopardy! (1964–1975; 1978–79)

Host for the original version, Fleming declined to host the comeback in 1983. His friend Pat Sajak took the job.

Jack Narz ➤◄ Concentration (1973–78)

Dennis James ➤◄ The Price Is Right (1972–77)

Jim Perry ➤◄ $ale of the Century (1983–89)

John Davidson ➤◄ Hollywood Squares (1986–89)

Ray Combs ➤◄ Family Feud (1988–1994)

Mike Adamle ➤◄ American Gladiators (1989–1996)

TV News Anchors of the Seventies and Eighties

The explosion in cable channels that began with CNN in 1980 brought a host of fresh presenters to join the ranks of trusted personalities that bring us the news. How many of them do you remember?

Dan Rather ♟ (CBS)
"Kenneth, what's the frequency?" Those were the words of the man who attacked Rather in 1986. It took a decade before the message was decoded; his assailant wanted to block the beams he believed TV networks were using to target him.

Peter Jennings ♟ (ABC)
Tom Brokaw ♟ (NBC)
Ted Koppel ♟ (ABC)
Bill Beutel ♟ (ABC)
Jessica Savitch ♟ (NBC)
Connie Chung ♟ (NBC)
Diane Sawyer ♟ (CBS/ABC)
Sam Donaldson ♟ (ABC)
Barbara Walters ♟ (ABC)
Walters was a popular pioneer; the first woman to co-host and anchor news programs, reaching 74 million viewers with her interview of Monica Lewinsky.

Frank Reynolds ♟ (ABC)
Jane Pauley ♟ (NBC)
Roger Grimsby ♟ (ABC)
Roger Mudd ♟ (CBS/NBC)
Garrick Utley ♟ (NBC)
Bernard Shaw ♟ (CNN)
Frank McGee ♟ (NBC)
Ed Bradley ♟ (CBS)
Larry King ♟ (CNN)
Kathleen Sullivan ♟ (ABC/CBS/NBC)
Jim Lehrer ♟ (PBS)
Robert MacNeil ♟ (PBS)
In 1963, MacNeil had a brief exchange of words with a man leaving the Texas School Book Depository; to this day, it is uncertain whether this was Lee Harvey Oswald.

FIFA World Cup: Down to the Last Four in Your Life

Here are the teams that have made the last four of the world's most watched sporting event in your lifetime (last year in brackets). The US men's team has reached the semifinals once, back in 1930.

France ⚽ (2018, winner)
Croatia ⚽ (2018, runner-up)
During a 2006 match against Australia, Croatian player Josip Šimunić was booked three times due to a referee blunder.

Belgium ⚽ (2018, 3rd)
England ⚽ (2018, 4th)
In the run-up to the 1966 World Cup the trophy was stolen and held to ransom. An undercover detective met the crook with fake banknotes and he was arrested; a dog named Pickles found the trophy under a bush.

Brazil ⚽ (2014, 4th)
Germany ⚽ (2014, winner)
Argentina ⚽ (2014, runner-up)
Netherlands ⚽ (2014, 3rd)
Spain ⚽ (2010, winner)
Uruguay ⚽ (2010, 4th)
Italy ⚽ (2006, winner)
Portugal ⚽ (2006, 4th)
Turkey ⚽ (2002, 3rd)
Korean Republic ⚽ (2002, 4th)
Sweden ⚽ (1994, 3rd)
Bulgaria ⚽ (1994, 4th)
Poland ⚽ (1982, 3rd)
Russia ⚽ (1966, 4th)
Czech Republic (as Czechoslovakia) ⚽ (1962, runner-up)
Chile ⚽ (1962, 3rd)
The 1962 World Cup saw the 'Battle of Santiago' between Chile and Italy. The first foul occurred 12 seconds into the game, a player was punched in the nose, and police intervened several times.

Serbia (as Yugoslavia) ⚽ (1962, 4th)

Books of the Decade

Our final decade of books are the bookstore favorites from your fifties. How many did you read...and can you remember the plot, or the cover?

2006	The Secret by Rhonda Byrne
2006	Eat, Pray, Love by Elizabeth Gilbert
2006	The Road by Cormac McCarthy
2007	A Thousand Splendid Suns by Khaled Hosseini
2007	City of Bones by Cassandra Clare
2008	The Hunger Games by Suzanne Collins
2008	The Girl with the Dragon Tattoo by Stieg Larsson
2009	Catching Fire by Suzanne Collins
2009	The Lost Symbol by Dan Brown
2009	The Help by Kathryn Stockett
2010	The Girl Who Kicked the Hornets' Nest by Stieg Larsson
2010	Mockingjay by Suzanne Collins
2010	Freedom by Jonathan Franzen
2011	Fifty Shades of Grey by E.L. James
2011	The Best of Me by Nicholas Sparks
2011	Divergent by Veronica Roth
2012	Gone Girl by Gillian Flynn
2012	Me Before You by Jojo Moyes
2013	The Tenth of December by George Saunders
2013	Inferno by Dan Brown
2014	All the Light We Cannot See by Anthony Doerr
2014	The Goldfinch by Donna Tartt
2015	The Girl on the Train by Paula Hawkins
2015	The Nightingale by Kristin Hannah

April 17, 1970: Jim Lovell is brought aboard a helicopter—the last of the three astronauts from the Apollo 13 mission to be lifted from the floating Command Module.

Apollo Astronauts

Whatever your personal memories of the events, the moon landings are now woven into our national story—but not all of the Apollo astronauts who made the journey are equally well known. Twelve landed; twelve remained in lunar orbit. Gus Grissom, Ed White, and Roger B Chaffee died in training.

Landed on the moon:

Alan Bean

Alan Shepard

Shepard was the oldest person to walk on the moon at age 47.

Buzz Aldrin

Charles Duke

David Scott

Edgar Mitchell

Eugene Cernan

Harrison Schmitt

James Irwin

John Young

Neil Armstrong

Pete Conrad

Remained in low orbit:

Al Worden

Bill Anders

Anders took the iconic "Earthrise" photo.

Dick Gordon

Frank Borman

Fred Haise

Jack Swigert

Jim Lovell

Ken Mattingly

Michael Collins

Ron Evans

Made the final spacewalk of the program to retrieve film cassettes.

Stuart Roosa

On the Apollo 14 mission he carried seeds from 5 species of trees. They were planted across the US and are known as "Moon Trees."

Tom Stafford

US Open Tennis

And now it's the women's turn. Here are the tournament's victors when you were between the ages of the current "winning window": 16 years (Tracy Austin in 1979), and a venerable 42 years (Molla Mallory in 1926: she won eight times).

1971–72	Billie Jean King
1973	**Margaret Court**

In 1973, the US Open became the first Grand Slam tournament to offer equal prize money to male and female winners.

1974	Billie Jean King
1975–78	**Chris Evert**

During the 1975 US Open, Evert beat her long-time rival Martina Navratilova in the semi-final. That evening, Navratilova defected to the United States.

1979	Tracy Austin
1980	Chris Evert
1981	Tracy Austin
1982	Chris Evert
1983–84	Martina Navratilova
1985	Hana Mandikova
1986–87	**Martina Navratilova**

All four US Open finalists in 1986 (two male and two female) were born in Czechoslovakia.

1988–89	Steffi Graf
1990	Gabriela Sabatini
1991–92	Monica Seles
1993	Steffi Graf
1994	Arantxa Sanchez Vicario
1995–96	Steffi Graf
1997	**Martina Hingis**

16-year-old Hingis defeated 17-year-old Venus Williams in the youngest Grand Slam tournament final of the Open era.

1998	Lindsay Davenport

Things People Did When You Were Growing Up (Part 2)

Finally, here are more of the things we did and errands we ran as kids that nobody needs, wants, or even understands how to do in the modern age!

✦ Buy cigarettes for your parents at the corner store as a child
✦ Use a pay phone (there was one on almost every corner)
✦ Join a bowling league
✦ Collect cigarette or baseball trading cards
✦ Get frozen meals delivered to your door by the iconic refrigerated yellow Schwan's truck
✦ Attend "Lawn Faiths"/ ice cream socials
✦ Chat with strangers over CB radio
✦ Look up a phone number in the Yellow or White Pages
✦ Visit the Bookmobile for new library books
✦ Have a radio repaired at an appliance/electronics shop
✦ Ride your bike without a helmet
✦ Go to American Bandstand parties
✦ Take part in a panty raid prank
✦ Attend a sock hop
✦ Get milk delivered to your door
✦ Hang out with friends at a pizzeria
✦ Use a rotary phone at home
✦ Use a typewriter
✦ Save your term paper on a floppy disc
✦ Listen to LPs and the newest 45s
✦ Care for a pet rock
✦ Use a card catalogue to find books at the library
✦ Attend a Sadie Hawkins Dance where girls invited the boys
✦ Go disco roller skating